# SOME MAKERS OF THE MODERN SPIRIT

# SOME MAKERS OF THE
# MODERN SPIRIT

## A SYMPOSIUM

EDITED BY

## JOHN MACMURRAY

*Essay Index Reprint Series*

BOOKS FOR LIBRARIES PRESS

FREEPORT, NEW YORK

First Published 1933
Reprinted 1968

LIBRARY OF CONGRESS CATALOG CARD NUMBER:
68-22926

PRINTED IN THE UNITED STATES OF AMERICA

# CONTENTS

PREFACE

# PREFACE

THIS book consists of the series of twelve talks entitled 'Some Makers of the Modern Spirit' which was arranged by the British Broadcasting Corporation and broadcast in the spring of 1933. They are introduced by the pamphlet on 'The Modern Spirit' which was originally published in connexion with the series. In publishing the series of talks in book form an effort has been made to keep the talks as much as possible in the form in which they were originally delivered. Minor changes have been made to suit the demands of literary presentation, but the substance has not been interfered with. It is inevitable that there should remain obvious traces of the influence of the original purpose of the material. More substantial alterations would have destroyed the value of the book as a permanent record of an effort in educational broadcasting which excited considerable public interest.

One result of this is that it is more than usually important to emphasize that the contributions of the different authors concerned are independent of one another and that each is responsible only for what he himself has written and in no sense for views expressed by any of the others. The account, for example, which Father D'Arcy would have given of the medieval world or of the work of Luther would differ radically from the views actually expressed by Mr. Micklem or myself. No attempt has been made to secure a common point of view.

This does not mean, however, that the book does not form a unity. Each contributor has expressed his own view on the subject allotted to him with full regard to the plan of the series as a whole. This plan was to present in historical order some of the main ideas which have been woven together in the course of the last centuries to form the pattern of the modern spirit. To this end the diversity of outlook represented by the various contributors is essential, for it is of first importance that a historical person and the ideas for which he stood should be presented by some one who is at least in general sympathy with them.

I should like to take this opportunity to thank the British Broadcasting Corporation for their readiness to facilitate the publication of the talks in book form.

JOHN MACMURRAY

University College, London
*June 9th,* 1933

## THE MODERN SPIRIT

### By John Macmurray

*Grote Professor of the Philosophy of Mind and Logic,
University of London*

THE chapters which follow will be mainly concerned with the lives, ideas and work of outstanding individuals. This introductory essay, however, has been written as a kind of inner history of the modern world with little attention to the personalities in whose lives and thought the development was embodied. Such a history of the evolution of the modern spirit will, of course, be an individual one, and to some extent subjective. It is unlikely that all the contributors or all readers will agree with it. It is even desirable that they should not. Its main function is to represent the long process of the growth of thought as a unity with a pattern of its own, and that can be best achieved by providing one possible interpretation, and by making it as clear and simple as it can be made. It will then form a framework within which the particular elements of the modern spirit which we are to consider can be fitted together and seen in relation to one another. Without such a framework of interpretation, the interrelation of the different chapters, and the unity of the whole series would never appear at all. With it, even if it is an unsatisfactory interpretation, the unity of purpose in the series will be revealed, and a basis will be provided for discussion, whether by way of agreement or disagreement.

The essay should be read, therefore, as an account of the way in which I myself find it possible to interpret the historical process in the modern world which has resulted in the production of that outlook upon the world and upon life which, in spite of all superficial differences, is common to us all, and which, for that reason, we call the modern spirit. Those who disagree with my interpretation—and no doubt they will be many—may still be able to use it as a valuable aid to defining a different interpretation which will satisfy them.

## THE MEDIEVAL MATRIX OF THE MODERN SPIRIT

We must realize from the outset that the modern spirit is not self-contained. Historically, it is the spirit which has developed in Western Europe since the breakdown of the medieval world, and which has spread with increasing rapidity in the last century over the whole world. But it is not a completely new creation. It is continuous with the medieval spirit out of which it developed, and in some of its aspects it is still thoroughly medieval. The development, too, has been a slow one, though the rate of change has become much greater in recent years. We must represent the growth of the modern spirit as a gradual transformation of the medieval spirit which is not even yet complete. For this reason we must begin with the medieval spirit and go on to discover the successive stages by which it has been transformed into the spirit of the modern world. If we can do this, it will provide a clue to the changes which are going on in us at the present day, by showing how much remains still untransformed by the leaven which is at work within it, and which has partially succeeded in changing the character of the medieval consciousness in which the process began.

The medieval world was by no means a world of barbaric darkness waiting for the light of the modern spirit to dawn upon it. In its maturity it was much less barbarous than modern civilization. The future may hold the promise of a finer culture than that of medieval Europe at its best. But the past has nothing better to show. The present is, at best, an unfinished structure where it is hardly possible to see the building for the scaffolding.

The reason for taking this view of the medieval world is that in its maturity it was a complete culture. The elements of culture are all to be found in any developed civilization, but usually, as in our own day, they are isolated from one another, independent of one another, or even antagonistic and at war. The completeness of medieval culture lies in the fact that it achieved a unification of these. On the external side Europe was one in the Middle Ages in a way that it never has been since, in spite of the fact that the difficulties of communication were immense. Its religion, its scholarship, its art and philosophy, were one throughout its whole extent. On the inner side the various aspects of its culture were harmoniously combined. Religion, art and science, politics, morality, metaphysics, and theology, were all felt to be expressions of a single spirit which belonged equally to all men everywhere. They were not merely felt to be parts of a single whole, they worked as such with considerable effectiveness in practice. Nor was this great unity a mere blank uniformity. Local loyalties and national patriotisms, which voiced the sense of a multitude of differences in which the common life of Europe expressed itself, were even stronger and more assertive than they are to-day. But they were happier differences than ours because of the pervasive sense of a common spirit underlying and uniting them. It is true—though not the whole truth —and well worth remembering, that the unity of Europe which seems to us so necessary to achieve, yet too superhuman a task for our achievement, was once a fact, and that the warring and competing nations of modern Europe are merely the broken ruins of the medieval world.

This unity of culture was a religious unity. Religion, in fact, is that aspect of culture which alone can unify the human spirit, either in the individual or as a society of men. It is the absence of religion in the modern world that makes it impossible to achieve a human unity, for the external unity of a civilization can only be the outward expression of the inner unity of its spirit. It is this religious unity of culture which the medieval world achieved that we usually refer to as Christianity. It is the cultural tradition of the Western world, and it is because such culture as we still possess is inherited from the Middle Ages that we speak of the nations of Europe to this day as Christian nations. It is not without reason that when we think of our culture we turn our thoughts to the past and feel that it is a heritage which has come down to us, not a product of our own creative activity.

## CIVILIZATION AND CULTURE

The true product of the modern world is science, and the applications of science to the development of civilization. When we think of science we do not look to the past, but to the future. We do not feel it as an inheritance that has been bequeathed to us, but as a triumph of our own which is still only beginning to reveal its power to change the conditions of human life. This extension of our control over the conditions of life, and particularly its material conditions, is what we really mean by the progress of civilization. We find ourselves contrasting civilization and culture, and there is a real reason for doing so. Civilization has to do with the environment in which we live. Culture is concerned with life itself and the way it is lived. The contrast is not absolute. The two things are never completely separable. You cannot have a civilization with no culture, nor can you have a culture without some civilization. But the contrast is a real one for all that. You may have a highly-developed culture where civilization is still rather primitive, as you had in ancient Greece. Equally you may have a highly-developed civilization in which the culture is primitive, as was the case in the Roman Empire. One cannot, therefore, assume that because a society, like that of modern Europe, is highly civilized it must also have reached a correspondingly high degree of culture. In other words, it is possible to develop the capacity to control the conditions of human life without having developed the capacity to live life finely even under the most satisfactory conditions. Where this is so, it always means that there is a division or a disharmony in the spirit of society. It means that the different aspects of the inner life are not unified, and that means in its turn the absence of the unifying factor, which is religion.

Now, the inner factor through which the development of civilization, as distinct from culture, is achieved, is science in the widest sense of the term. It is obvious, at a first glance, that the development of science is the outstanding characteristic of the modern spirit. For this reason, the development of the modern world is primarily the development of civilization. It is a continuous increase in the capacity to control the conditions of human existence and in the application, in practice, of this capacity. It is not primarily a development of culture or of the capacity to live a truly human life. Any account that we give of the development of the modern world will be an account of its progress in civilization. It will not be primarily, perhaps not at all, an account of progress in culture, that is to say, of an improvement in the quality of human life itself.

## THE DISINTEGRATION OF EUROPEAN CULTURE

On the cultural side, taken in its full sweep and ignoring the ups and downs of history, the development of the modern spirit is the story of the gradual disintegration of the culture which the medieval world achieved. The Middle Ages accumulated a great spiritual fortune, which it bequeathed to the modern world. The modern world has been living on its capital ever since. This does not mean that there have been no cultural movements in Europe since the Middle Ages, nor that nothing of importance has been added to the world's culture during the history of the modern world. Quite the contrary. It means rather that the cultural life of the modern period has always been on the defensive, that it has been fighting a series of heroic but unsuccessful battles in defence of a heritage which has been slowly but surely slipping from its grasp. Not infrequently, the greatest achievements in warfare have been those of armies in retreat. So it has been in the history of the modern spirit. Civilization has been advancing steadily from victory to victory. Culture has been gradually driven from its fortified positions after a heroic resistance, until at last it is within sight of a final and overwhelming defeat. If we were seeking to estimate the heroism and human capacity shown in individual incidents during the long campaign, we should probably find that they were fairly evenly distributed between the soldiers of advancing civilization and those of retreating culture. But we are concerned with a different task. We have to understand the movement as a whole. From that point of view, we have to notice merely the steady progress of material civilization based upon science and the steady disintegration of a culture inherited from the past.

We must not imagine, however, that we are dealing with two unrelated movements. The advance of civilization and the disintegration of culture are two aspects of a single movement of the human spirit. For, in the first place, the development of science, which is the source of the advancing civilization, is itself an aspect of cultural progress, and if it looks, ultimately, to the control of conditions, it is itself maintained by cultural forces which aim at an increase in the quality of life itself. In the second place, the disintegration of culture is largely the result of the development of science. Not that science necessarily destroys culture or desires to destroy it. But it has inevitably destroyed the basis upon which the medieval culture which we inherited rests.

## Modern Science and Medieval Culture

The reason for this can be simply, if somewhat roughly, stated. Science is concerned with facts. Culture is concerned with values. When we are concerned to get at the facts about anything we have to hold in abeyance our capacities for appreciation and enjoyment. Like Browning's grammarian, we have

to decide ' not to live but know.' The preoccupation
of the modern spirit with the development of science
has meant that its energies have been withdrawn from
the appreciation of the world to the knowledge of it.
There is nothing here either to praise or to blame.
The task was set us by history. We have been the
makers of knowledge and the controllers of the conditions of life. But to be this we have been compelled
perforce to hold ourselves aloof from the activities by
which culture is created and to live, so far as we
were concerned to live, by a culture that we did not
make.

But value and fact cannot exist in complete separation
from one another. The values we live by are the
values of the world we know, and, therefore, the culture of the medieval world was inextricably bound up
with its beliefs about the nature of the world. The
effect of the development of science has been to show
that a great many of the beliefs about matters of fact
which formed the basis of the medieval culture were
not true. The scientific picture of the world which we
have achieved is very different from the picture of it
which men took for truth before science began. So,
little by little, the values which we inherited have got
cut loose from their basis in knowledge. This does
not necessarily mean that they have become false.
It does mean that they are divorced from the world
as we know it, and seem to have no points of contact
with the conditions under which our lives are lived.
They float like ghosts from another world over the
surface of our lives, fascinating and lovely, but somehow alien and unsubstantial. It is impossible to live
by them, even if we believe in them. Under such
conditions, they are bound to fade away. Beliefs
which have no means of making contact with practical
activity cannot persist indefinitely in our minds.

Thus, indirectly and unintentionally, by undermining the basis of fact to which medieval culture was attached, science has been the innocent cause of the gradual disintegration of modern culture.

## A Clue to the Problem

We have now got the key to the development of the modern spirit in our hands. The problem is to represent as simply as possible the general character of the movement of thought and feeling which has brought us from medievalism to the very different world in which we live. Starting from the balanced and harmonious culture of the medieval system and the rather primitive civilization on which it was based, we can trace a double line of continuous change. There has been a steady advance of scientific knowledge and, with it, of our power to control the conditions of life. The gradual application of this growing knowledge has meant a steady progress in civilization. This is the positive movement of the modern spirit. The other side of the picture is that the changes in our knowledge of the world have destroyed little by little the basis upon which our inherited culture was built, so that bit by bit it has been undermined. We have made efforts again and again to prop it up and to provide it with a new basis. But we have produced no new culture of our own upon the basis of the new knowledge that science has given us. The result is that our efforts have been unavailing, and in spite of all that has been done our culture has steadily declined. This is the negative movement in the development of the modern spirit, and I call it the disintegration of modern culture.

The whole movement falls into three distinct stages, two of which have been completed, while the third has recently begun.   In every stage, the positive and the negative movements in the development are closely correlated with one another.   The correlation between the development of science and the disintegration of culture is the result of the tension between the two movements.   Culture resists the attack upon the conception of the world which forms the foundation of the values by which it lives, and, therefore, seeks to prevent the development of scientific investigation altogether, or, when that has become impossible, seeks to limit the field within which scientific investigation is carried on.   There are two points to be noticed in this connexion.   The first is that there are some fields of knowledge which are more important than others from a cultural point of view.   Culture is concerned with the values by which we live.   And these values are grounded in our emotions.   Indeed, the culture of any society might be defined as the organization of its emotional life.   About some things it feels very strongly, about others less strongly, about some hardly at all.   And these distinctions in people's emotional outlook are relatively stable for any one society at a particular period, though they may vary greatly in different societies or at different periods.   There is, however, a general distinction which we can make that holds good everywhere and always.   Our emotions are much more strongly aroused by things that touch us personally and affect our personal life, than by things to which we are personally indifferent.   As a result, the personal field is always charged with emotion much more highly than the material field.   Between the two lies the field of life in its organic, impersonal aspect.   This field is more highly charged with significance for us than the field of matter, but less highly than the field of personality itself.

Now, the resistance which culture makes to the

inroads of the unbiassed, detached, unemotional investigations of science will be strongest where the emotional significance of what is investigated is highest. So, quite naturally, science will first be permitted to investigate the material world, but prevented, by the resistance of culture, from entering the fields of life and personality. Similarly, when it has forced its way into the field of organic life it will meet with concentrated resistance against a further advance into the field of personal life. As a result, the development of science falls into three stages. In the first stage, we find the development of the physical sciences which deal only with the material world. In the second stage, the field of life is included, and the biological sciences produced. But it is not until the third stage that science is able to carry its detached and impersonal investigation into the field of the personal and produce a scientific psychology.

We shall miss the full force of this analysis unless we remember that the forces which limit the field of scientific investigation are in people's minds ; indeed, they are just as much in the minds of the scientists as anywhere else. You cannot be scientific about anything until you can think about it without emotional excitement. If it excites your feelings it blinds your judgement. Very few people, for example, can think calmly enough at the present day about Bolshevism to form a cool judgement of it. They are either excited against it or in its favour. A great many people, too, are still unable to think calmly about modern psychology. Its results touch them too nearly, and throw their minds into a state in which a detached judgement is just impossible. These are examples of the way in which the forces of culture work to limit the field of science. They produce inhibitions in the mind.

Corresponding to these three stages in the development of science there are three stages in the disintegration of culture. Transitions from one stage to the next are marked by a break-down of the inhibitions which effectively limit the field in which science is free to operate in the earlier stage. Until these inhibitions are broken down science cannot advance into a new field. The breaking down of such a set of inhibitions inevitably means that some aspect of the traditional culture has lost its hold over the modern spirit. For it means that at last men can be calm and impersonal about things which up till then had excited their emotions. That is why the three stages of the scientific advance are also three stages in the disintegration of traditional culture.

## SCIENCE AND CULTURE

Does this mean that science and culture are incompatible? Is it inevitable that the advance of science must destroy our emotional appreciation of the value and significance of the world? I do not think so for a moment. The reason why our science is gradually destroying our culture lies only in the fact that our particular culture is incompatible with scientific knowledge. It is incompatible because it is not really ours. It is only inherited from an age when science was unknown, and when it was an integral part of a conception of the world and of a form of civilization which science has destroyed. It is quite possible that when the future has developed a new culture on the basis of our scientific knowledge of the world, that new culture will not be essentially different from the old one which science has destroyed. It may value human life and organize human emotions in much the same way. I do not say that it will, but it might.

The difference would be that the new valuations
would be unified with the scientific picture of the
world, instead of being up in the air like a city in
the clouds detached from their basis in our scientific
knowledge of the foundations, the conditions, and the
mechanism of life.

But there is another reason why our traditional
culture is incompatible with science. It is an unconscious culture. By this I mean that it grew up without
deliberate human effort, unintentionally, as an adjustment to the conditions of life in the Middle Ages.
Palestine, Greece, and Rome, as well as the primitive
peoples of Europe in whose minds the medieval culture
grew up, all contributed their traditional conceptions
of life to the melting-pot. Somehow, these heterogeneous contributions were fused in the cauldron of
affliction during the long centuries that we describe
as the Dark Ages. Slowly, as life cooled down, this
mass of molten tradition crystallized out in the form
that we know. No one really knew why he believed
or felt or behaved as he did. The force that maintained these beliefs and feelings was the force of the
fused tradition which had moulded itself in a way
that was felt to be satisfactory to the conditions of
medieval civilization. Truth and value were both
guaranteed by traditional authority. Men thought
and felt as they did simply because that was the way
that they were accustomed to think and feel. Any
question was met immediately by the appeal to
authority, and the authority itself was the guardian
of tradition. The great work of the Middle Ages,
which employed all the talents of its great men—and
some of them were very great men—was this synthesis
of tradition. It was not concerned with the criticism
of tradition and the discovery of something unknown.
Its task was to fit the heterogeneous elements which

had come down to it from many sources into a single homogeneous whole. In the process some of these elements had to go, because they could not be fitted in. Others had to be whittled into shape to make them fit. But what governed the formation of the medieval culture was always and primarily the need to unify beliefs and emotions which it found in existence. It was not the pressure of an urgent need to know whether these beliefs and emotions were true and real.

Science, on the other hand, is not something that grows of itself. It is a highly conscious and deliberate activity. The civilization that is based upon it has to be conscious and deliberate too. The modern spirit is not interested, like the medieval, primarily in the unification of beliefs. It is interested in taking them to pieces to find out if they are true. It is interested also in using the truth that it discovers, piece-meal and bit by bit, to enable it to plan and control the conditions of life. That is why the advance of science brings with it the need of more and more planning and deliberate foresight in every field of individual and social activity. The unconscious character of the culture we have inherited, with its emphasis on tradition, and so on the maintenance of beliefs and attitudes of mind, is thus in opposition with the scientific spirit, which is careless whether it destroys beliefs if only it can get at the truth. This, perhaps, is the main reason why the advance of science has involved the disintegration of culture in the modern world.

## WHAT SCIENCE OWES TO THE MIDDLE AGES

Having discovered our clue to the development of the modern spirit, we must now run through the stages

of the development itself, beginning with the Middle
Ages. The medieval culture was the culmination of
a long process of human experience, but it was also
the starting-point of the modern world. We must
look at it now from this point of view, looking forward
from it rather than backward to it. From this point
of view we see that what the Middle Ages did was
to create the form of thought upon which science
depends. If we look at the work of a great thinker
like St. Thomas Aquinas we shall be amazed by the
subtlety and the comprehensiveness of his thought.
It embraces everything in heaven and earth, and
presents it in a single system of theory in which everything has its own place and nothing is left out. There
are no loose ends anywhere. The network of logical
connexion binds everything together in a hierarchy
of ordered forms. Here we have pure thought at its
very best, combining the utmost comprehensiveness
with an extreme clarity both in the organization and
in the expression of ideas. It is probably true to say
that the philosophy of St. Thomas stands unrivalled
in human history as an expression of what a mind can
achieve as a pure thinking machine. It is the supreme
intellectual expression of medieval culture. On the
other hand, it is a formal achievement. St. Thomas
did not discover the beliefs that he expresses. He
organized the beliefs which had grown up, as the
result of the process of tradition, into a single system
of orderly thought. In doing so, of course, he clarified
the tradition and brought it into the full light of consciousness. That is, indeed, the function of pure thought.

For reasons which we need not discuss here people's
interests began to shift at the end of the Middle Ages
from form to content. I mean, for example, that they
began to doubt whether the traditional beliefs and the
traditional organization of life which these beliefs

sustained were really true. First one belief and then another was doubted. And the very fact that the organization of these beliefs was so complete meant that if one was proved false the whole system to which it belonged was shaken. That was the beginning of the modern world. Instead of accepting beliefs because they were customary, on the basis of traditional authority, men began to ask: ' How can we discover whether what we have been accustomed to believe is really true?' Once that question is asked, there is no going back on it. Europe was committed to the criticism of its traditional beliefs.

But even if doubt is thrown upon the whole content of belief in such a system of thought, something remains —the form of its organization. St. Thomas Aquinas had taught the world the organizing capacity of thought. He had also exhibited the universal form which any system of thought must take if it is to be complete and satisfactory, whatever may be the particular beliefs which enter into it. He had taught men to think of the universe as a single system of interrelated parts governed by a single law. When the modern world began to doubt the beliefs which the Middle Ages had organized in that way it did not doubt the form of their organization. It set out to discover for itself a set of beliefs which could be accepted consciously and deliberately and to organize them, as it discovered them, in the same form. Behind all the activities of science lies this conception of the uniformity of Nature and of the universality of law. Even when it cuts out God as the lawgiver, science still talks of matter obeying laws, and even when it confesses that it can give no explanation of the system and order in the world, even when it is driven to say that it merely happened somehow, it still insists, like Thomas Aquinas, that the world must be through and through systematic, orderly and law-abiding. Even if we moderns are determined that we must find out for ourselves *what* we are to believe, it was the Middle Ages that taught us *how* we must believe if our beliefs are not to fight one another frantically and ruin our sanity. Our beliefs, whatever they are, must not be disorderly. They must be systematic and unified.

## The Descent into Humanism

The disintegration of the medieval culture shows itself first in the development of individualism. Individualism is simply the self-assertion of the individual. In a society which is unified by tradition, the individual is not self-conscious. He behaves spontaneously as a member of the group to which he belongs because he shares its habits of thought and never thinks of questioning its customs. He may break its rules, but if he does he knows that he is doing what he should not do, even if he enjoys his own wickedness. There is no self-assertion in this. But when a man consciously departs from the tradition of his society in action or belief, and feels that he is right in doing so, or that he has a right to do so if he wishes, then he has asserted himself as an individual. It is, indeed, only when a man does this that he becomes self-conscious. Individualism, therefore, involves a tension between two things, the individual acting consciously in his own way on his own initiative and a tradition which demands that he should act in another way. This tension, we should remember, is in the mind of the individual himself. The tradition is his own habit of acting which he shares with every one else, so that individualism can only exist where there is a struggle between our own tendency to follow tradition and our own desire to assert ourselves. In a society where every one naturally follows tradition, or accepts its authority completely, individualism is unknown. And in a society where every one naturally lived by his own decisions, and where every one recognized his right to do so, there could be no individualism either. Individualism is, in fact, a half-and-half condition of the human mind in which half our consciousness is on the side of authority and half of it on the side of freedom. Naturally, it is characteristic of the whole modern world, because of the struggle between a traditional culture and the development of scientific civilization which has gone on continuously from the end of the Middle Ages to the present day.

The appearance of individualism on a large scale towards the end of the Middle Ages must mean, therefore, that the hold of tradition and authority over men's minds is weakening. This weakening of the force of tradition produced the movement which is called in history the Renaissance. Looking at it from this point of view, we may trace the movement a long way back into the Middle Ages. Perhaps its real origin is to be found in the life and work of St. Francis of Assisi, and the impulse which he gave to activities in art and thought, as well as in social and religious action, which are not purely traditional. The culmination of the Renaissance was the Protestant Reformation, and Luther's open defiance of the Pope. It is noteworthy, though not at all surprising, that both these men are religious figures. For the central point of the medieval culture was religious, and it was the religious character of its culture which made it the comprehensive unity that it was. We may put this in another way by saying that the central authority which guaranteed the unity of medieval culture was the authority of the Church. That, however, is an external point of view. It was not the authority of the

Church that maintained the unity of culture, but the acceptance of that authority by everybody as unquestionable. It was the unquestioning belief in God, which was part of the mental make-up of every one, that guaranteed the authority of the Church and of tradition. Just because medieval culture is unified by the belief in God, it can stand so long as that belief retains its hold over the emotions of men. The disintegration of medieval culture must, therefore, begin with the questioning of its divine sanction and its religious tradition. It was not until the growing individualism of the Renaissance reached the point at which it could challenge effectively the authority of the Church that the modern world could really begin. You had first to have *religious* individualism, and for that people had to reach the point at which they could defy religious tradition and feel that they were right in defying it. That is why the Protestant Reformation marks the beginning of the modern world. With the Reformation the unity of the medieval culture has been broken, and its disintegration has begun.

We can now see the importance of Luther in the history of the modern spirit. He was the first man to assert himself on religious grounds, and successfully, against the authority of tradition in religion. In doing that he struck a blow at the heart of the medieval culture. The particular religious beliefs which he proposed to put in the place of the traditional religion are a matter of much less consequence. What does matter is that he destroyed the unity of Europe by successfully asserting his right to determine his religious beliefs for himself. Some people might say that he merely inaugurated a new religious tradition which was no better than the old one, perhaps not so good. That may be true, but it misses the point. The real point is that he set his own conviction against the whole authority of religious tradition, and that his action awakened such a widespread response in the hearts of men that the authority of tradition was unable to silence it.  He established the central thesis of the modern spirit, the right of the individual to worship God in his own way.  Once that right of the individual was established the medieval culture was doomed. Its disintegration was merely a matter of time.  It could not even be re-established, for the simple reason that it depended upon the fact that no one had thought of challenging it.  It was unconscious.  Any effort to re-establish medievalism in the modern world would be a conscious and deliberate effort, which would be based upon the very individualism which it aimed at destroying.

The first stage of the disintegration of medieval culture, which is typified in the life and work of Luther, is a descent into humanism.  By this I mean that, whereas in Aquinas, for example, it is God who is in the centre of the picture, with Luther it is man.  No doubt Luther did not mean this.  For all that, it was the inevitable effect of his action upon the traditional culture.  If Luther could have established a religion which was *not* traditional he might have escaped this result.  But that was impossible.  All that he could do was to assert the right of the human individual to choose to reject whatever he found unacceptable in the religious tradition of Europe.  If you follow the history of Protestantism you will find that as time goes on more and more of the tradition is rejected.  And it is rejected on the ground that men can no longer believe it.  Religion has been submitted to human judgement.  That is what I mean when I say that the Reformation put man in the centre of the picture. Religion becomes itself a human thing, one of the activities of man.

In the first stage of modern development, therefore, culture is humanist. Man and his activities have the central significance. Instead of man being significant in terms of God, God is now significant in terms of man. One of the simplest ways of indicating this is to draw attention to the change which comes over political thought and feeling. In the Middle Ages, men thought that the justification for government was to be found in the will of God. In the modern world, we think that it is to be found in the will of the people. That is a good illustration of the descent into humanism.

Some people might think that this represents an advance and not a descent to a lower level. I agree that it represents an advance in human development, but from the point of view of traditional culture it is undoubtedly a deterioration. God is one, and so can serve as a real centre of reference. But man is not one but many. It is only in idea that there is such a thing as Man. And unfortunately there may be as many ideas about Man as there are men to have them. This is the fatal defect of humanism. It cannot unify men and so achieve real community among them. The self-assertion of the individual, carried to its logical conclusion, can only mean the isolation of individuals from one another, each asserting himself against all the others. Obviously, such a conclusion could never be reached. Long before it had been achieved, life would have become impossible as well as intolerable. When culture becomes humanistic the necessary unification of life must be accomplished, not by culture, but by external means. If men are not united by an inner bond they will have to be united by an external pressure—by force, even if it is only the force of circumstances.

## THE FOUNDATIONS OF MECHANISM

Now, an external force is a mechanical force and, therefore, the descent of culture to the level of humanism, because it breaks the inner unity which binds men together into a society, compels men to re-establish the unity upon a mechanical basis. A mechanical force is simply a force which maintains unity by external pressure ; and in society, therefore, mechanism is the necessary consequence of individualism. When the Reformation established individualism and so originated the struggle of the modern spirit for the freedom of the individual, it also established mechanism as the temper which must accompany that struggle. As individual freedom is gradually achieved in the development of the modern world society becomes gradually more and more mechanical in its organization. The inner side of this development is the foundation and growth of modern science, and its application to the organization of social life.

Science begins as an interest in the mechanism of the material world. That in itself is an expression of individualism, for it involves a break with tradition. It means that men have begun to doubt the adequacy of traditional knowledge, to realize their own ignorance, and to believe that they can find out how the world works for themselves. In the long run, this interest in how things work will be extended to cover the whole field of experience, including the working of our own minds. But in the first stage the traditional culture is too strong to allow men to think scientifically—that is to say, mechanically—about anything but the material world. Until the tradition of humanism is in turn broken, science can only investigate matter. During the first stage of the modern development, therefore, the material sciences alone are established. The material world is treated as a mechanism. But life and mind are still considered in the traditional way, religiously.

It must not be thought that the physical sciences were created at a stroke. The process was indeed very prolonged. The scientists had to struggle for a long time against the forces of tradition for the right to carry on their investigation unhindered. Even when they achieved this freedom, their own minds were pervaded by traditional attitudes and traditional conceptions of the world. It was only gradually that they discovered what they were really after. Their results consisted largely in the discovery of isolated facts which, though they proved the falsity of traditional theories, did not suffice to produce any general theory to take the place of the old conception. They were also engaged in the manufacture of tools for their trade, not merely physical tools like the telescope, but intellectual tools, in particular new methods of mathematical analysis. It was the invention of the calculus—the credit of which is due to two men, Leibniz and Newton—which made possible a unification of the facts which earlier gropings had brought to light, and the establishment of a general theory of the material world as a mechanism. The event which marks this achievement is Newton's discovery of the law of gravitation. Previous to this discovery, all conceptions of the material universe as a single system of mechanical action were merely speculative. The law of gravitation, and its verification in terms of the known facts, brought the mechanical conception of the world out of the cloudy region of metaphysics and established it on the firm basis of scientific experiment. It was Newton, therefore, who finally established the mechanistic theory of matter. Before Newton, theory

This claim struck at the heart of humanist culture because it denied that the differences between men, differences of ability, of training, or of social position, could form a rational basis for the social order. Indeed, the demand for equality illustrates the progress that has been made by the idea of mechanism. Culture cannot be mechanical. It depends upon the natural harmony of differences. The humanist culture is possible only where the idea of a natural harmony between men of different types, of different abilities, of different rank and authority, is recognized. To base freedom on the equality of all individuals is to strike at the roots of humanism. Humanism cannot be democratic.

That, however, is the negative side of the cultural movement of Romanticism. On its positive side it turns from man to Nature, and thinks of man as one of the products of Nature, even if he is her highest product. Thus, the ' back-to-Nature' movement is a movement away from man as the centre of significance and interest. Just as the Reformation shifted the focus of culture from God and brought man into the centre of the picture, so the Romantic Revival in turn pushed humanity out of the centre of the picture and brought Nature into focus. The French Revolution, which followed closely upon Rousseau's death, marked in an unmistakable way the success of this movement and the disintegration of humanism.

There is no need for me to labour this point. We are all familiar with naturalism. One has only to take up a volume—any volume—of the poetry which the Romantic Revival produced to see how central the idea of Nature has become, and how human life has faded into its natural background and become an integral part of the greater life of Nature. What we are apt to miss is the relation of this to the whole culture of the nineteenth century and particularly to its social and political developments. Its connexion with democracy we have seen. But it meant equally the development of an interest in history, and particularly in primitive life in all its aspects. Already in Rousseau, we see it leading to the worship of childhood and the apotheosis of the ' noble savage,' for the simple reason that children and primitive peoples are nearer to Nature than civilized adults. This in turn has important practical consequences. The interest in childhood meant the beginnings of the education movements.

The interest in the primitive gave a great impetus to exploration and colonization, and brought about the efforts of the churches and of the industrialists and of governments to bring the backward peoples of the world within the orbit of civilization. On another side, the emphasis on Nature meant inevitably an emphasis upon the natural functions of life. By emphasizing growth it led to the idea of progress, an idea which reduces the significance of human life, whether individual or social, to the contribution which it makes to the future. This brings out clearly how incompatible the idea of progress is with humanism. For the latter is based upon the feeling that human life is significant in itself, absolutely, and not in relation to something beyond itself to which it contributes. But where progress is the central idea in social culture it inevitably reduces the individual to a level of significance where he is merely valuable because of the function he performs in society. That is the price we have had to pay for democracy in order to achieve equality as individuals. We have had to surrender our significance as human beings and become functions in the social organism. Even in the most personal and intimate relations between individuals this subordination to Nature makes its appearance. Marriage, for example, becomes natural rather than human, based upon the natural urge of sex and maintained for its social value, rather than as an expression of human relationship.

The development of this second stage in the disintegration of traditional culture falls into two parts, which we might call the idealist phase and the realist phase. The reason for this is that it is impossible for human beings to find the significance of their lives in Nature without idealizing or sentimentalizing Nature in the process. We may find our own significance in God or in ourselves, in that which is above us or on our own level in the order of things, without doing violence to the nature of reality. But when we look to that which is less than ourselves for the meaning of human life we must inevitably falsify it and deceive ourselves. That is why we have come to use the word romantic to mean illusory, and to talk about ' romancing ' when we mean telling lies. In the idealist phase of romantic culture this fatal flaw in naturalism is unrealized. The emphasis on Nature and on natural emotion is balanced unconsciously by the traditional inhibitions and the persistence of the very humanism which is being repudiated. We find, therefore, at the beginning of the nineteenth century, great figures, like Wordsworth or Goethe, in whom there is expressed a happy balance between the legacy of humanism and the new romantic naturalism. It is this that makes Goethe stand out as a universal figure, curiously detached from the immediate circumstances of his time. Yet if we look closer we shall find that all the elements which characterize romantic culture and distinguish it from the earlier humanism are perfectly expressed in his life and work. At the centre of it lies an almost religious reverence for Nature in all her forms and expressions. It is his human capacity to grasp them all and to balance them harmoniously that produces the impression of a universality which is tied to no particular period of human history.

But as the period progresses a doubt begins to set in. The more you study Nature, the more she appears to be indifferent to human values. Tennyson sees Nature ' red in tooth and claw,' and ' faintly trusts the larger hope.' People discover that romantic love is apt to work out in tragedy, and that progress seems to be driven by the greed of gain rather than by a love of humanity. Democracy fails to produce the Utopia which was expected of it. The only thing that seems to increase is wealth and power ; but it increases very unequally, so that it has a seamy side in a corresponding progress in poverty and squalor. Disillusionment on a wide scale begins to find a voice. This is the second phase, the realist phase, of naturalistic culture.

In its realist phase, naturalism falls back more and more upon the development of science. Disillusioned with the immediate results of progress, it consoles itself with hopes of the future, and looks to scientific development to make its dream come true in time. To do this it has to restate itself, as it were, to remind itself that Nature works slowly through gradual processes which may be painful and discouraging in order to reach a distant goal. So it applies the idea of growth to man himself, and begins to dream of a future in which man will have developed sufficiently to give a real significance to human life.

It is at this point that Nietzsche comes on the stage with his doctrine of the superman. Nietzsche himself is not so well known in this country as he deserves to be. We know him only through more intellectual and more scientific expressions like the works of George Bernard Shaw. On the Continent Nietzsche is known everywhere as the evangelist of a new gospel which is in fact a completer and more whole-hearted version of naturalistic culture. The early naturalism had been optimistic about man. He had only to change the conditions of life and throw off the yoke of a few traditional tyrannies to reveal himself in his true colours as the final and perfect achievement of Nature's creative artistry. So Rousseau proposed to 'take man as he is and States as they ought to be.' Nietzsche, on the other hand, has realized that man as he is is pretty poor stuff, only a half-finished article in Nature's workshop. We are merely a transition to man as he will be, the superman, for whom is reserved the enjoyment of the promises which romantic idealism had held out to man as he is. Freedom is still the goal, and it is still to be achieved by throwing over the shackles of tradition and living a free life of natural impulse. The difference is that Nietzsche has realized that the struggle is not one between the natural man and external circumstances, but a struggle within man himself between the impulse to freedom and the fear of freedom which makes us distrust our natural impulses and cling to tradition to save us from ourselves. So naturalism in its disillusionment rebels against democracy and equality, and stands by the real processes of natural growth, by the struggle for existence and the survival of the fittest. For Nietzsche, 'the fittest' means the man who has the natural courage to follow his impulse in defiance of tradition ; to assert the life in himself against the deadness of mechanism and of intellectualism, which is always the high priest of tradition. For it is always the few who have such courage, and it is they who are Nature's pathfinders to the superman whom she has planned and is still busy fashioning by the slow, ruthless, and often cruel methods which she employs.

## THE ADVANCE INTO BIOLOGY

In Nietzsche, romantic culture, in an effort to maintain itself, has really taken refuge in mysticism. It is struggling against the very process which had brought it into existence, and realizing that it must fail in the struggle. The real cause of this later phase of romanticism is the development of science in the biological field. The collapse of humanism destroyed the resistance of tradition that had confined science to the material world. A new phase of scientific development began. While it was groping towards the truth about living Nature, collecting facts, observing and comparing, and seeking for a unifying conception which would do for the science of life what Newton had done for the science of matter, it was still possible to idealize and sentimentalize about Nature. But when Darwin, about the middle of the nineteenth century, produced his theory of the origin of species by natural selection, based upon a mass of carefully tested evidence, biological science, in its turn, was established. The theory of evolution which had been in the air and growing in popularity for nearly a century ceased to be a speculative theory which could be used for the support of romantic illusions and was anchored firmly to fact. For the first time, it was possible to see life in its whole process as a single unity and to see it scientifically. For Darwin provided, not a speculative idea of progress, but a scientific hypothesis, which could be tested and verified. And it was—this is the important point—a mechanical hypothesis. It was no longer possible to have rosy visions of progress which flattered our all-too-human prejudices. Before Darwin, people believed in evolution, but it was a romantic belief in the inevitable

progress of life towards Utopia and the satisfaction
of human desire.  The effect of Darwin was to bring
evolution down from the clouds of vision into the
world of actuality.  The popular version of Darwinism,
however inaccurate it may be from an intellectual
point of view, does represent its inevitable cultural
and emotional significance.  ' After all, we are only
highly developed monkeys.'

The cultural reaction to Darwinism, particularly in
the field of religious tradition, is too well known to
need repetition.  But the religious reaction merely
speeded up a process which had begun at the Reformation.  Religion was not in the centre of the picture.
The real effect of the establishment of biological
science was to make the destruction of romantic culture
inevitable.  The effect was immediate and worked
itself out very rapidly.  We are apt to exaggerate the
speed of historical processes which are distant in time.
Ten years in the immediate past seems longer to us
than a century of medieval history.  We must avoid
this illusion.  Only fifty-five years elapsed between
the publication of Darwin's *Origin of Species* and the
outbreak of the Great War ; and the War brought the
second stage of the modern development to an end.
The cult of Nature could not survive the unprejudiced
investigation of biological facts.

### PROGRESS AND CIVILIZATION

There is, however, a side of the picture which we
have not yet sketched in.  The descent into naturalism,
while it opened the biological field to science, made it
possible also to apply the results of physical science
to the building up of a scientific civilization.  This
real progress in the control of the conditions of life
falls equally into two phases which are represented

in the chapters which follow by Bentham and Karl
Marx. They correspond to the social movements
usually referred to as individualism and socialism.
Neither of these movements is cultural. Both are
concerned with the reorganization of the social
conditions of life rather than with life itself.

This means, in the first place, that both these movements are concerned primarily with economic conditions. But while the first is concerned with the
economic freedom of the individual only, the second
is concerned with the equal economic freedom of all
individuals. Thus, they correspond to the two earlier
demands of the modern spirit which we have already
noted, the demand for individual freedom, which was
the heart of the Reformation, and the demand for
equality, which destroyed humanism and produced
the democratic revolutions. Applied to the control
of the conditions of life in society, the first produces
capitalism, while the second destroys capitalism in
order to produce the economic equality of socialism.
Capitalism and socialism represent, therefore, two
successive phases in the progress of civilization, corresponding to the two successive stages in the development
of the modern spirit. The two main ideas which
successively determined the inner movement of
European development are now successively applied
to the control of the conditions of life.

Bentham is probably best known as the founder of
utilitarianism rather than for his prodigious work for
social and legal reform. It was he who defined the
ideal of social organization as ' the greatest happiness
of the greatest number.' But he was under the
influence of the naturalistic fallacy. He belonged to
the early stages of the romantic culture. He thought,
therefore, sentimentally, that this could be achieved
by allowing the forces of natural growth full play in

the economic field. He stood for the freedom of the individual to compete without hindrance with other individuals in the development of industry. Out of this natural process he expected that the greatest happiness of the greatest number would emerge as an inevitable result. He idealized progress in the economic field, just as all the early romantics idealized progress in Nature. His followers carried this romantic theory much farther than Bentham himself. Like Goethe in the field of culture, Bentham showed a balance of mind and a universality of outlook which is largely due to the persistence of the humanist tradition acting as a brake upon the new naturalistic tendencies. But he is, for all that, the real source of the liberal tradition in the nineteenth century, of the policy of *laisser-faire* in economics, of utilitarianism in ethical, political, and social theory, and of the whole nineteenth-century individualist tradition. Whoever stands for capitalism against socialism, for the rights of private property against social control of the economic machine, for private initiative in industry against governmental regulation, is a Benthamite, whether he knows it or not.

Marx, on the other hand, represents the realist phase which results from the disintegration of romantic idealism. The idea of equality which produced romantic culture and the democratic revolution naturally produced also the socialist movement, but in its earlier form socialism was itself highly romantic and visionary, expressing an idealism which had never come to grips with facts. It was not until concrete experience of the natural processes of industrialism had deflated its idealism, until it became clear that the facts were against the theorists of inevitable progress towards the greatest happiness of the greatest number, that socialism really became a practical programme for the achievement of economic equality. It was

Marx who brought socialism down from the clouds into direct contact with economic facts. Marx, in fact, did for the theory of evolution in its application to the development of civilization precisely what Darwin had done for it in the biological field. He produced an evolutionary interpretation of social development which explained how it had been brought about by the play of universal natural forces acting upon countless numbers of individuals. As in the case of Darwin, the important point was, not that his hypothesis was true, but that it was a scientific hypothesis which could be tested, not by argument and logic, but by facts and experiment. For the first time, Marx made it possible to base the control of the conditions of civilized life upon a scientific theory of its natural process. He provided a working hypothesis, which could be modified and improved as experience increased, to guide the efforts of social reformers in the application of scientific knowledge to the planning and the control of the material conditions of human life. In making socialism scientific, Marx made it possible to plan its achievement. The demand for equality is inherent in democracy and firmly established in the modern spirit. It is difficult to believe that we could for long resist the demand for economic equality once it was shown convincingly to be practicable. That is why the whole world waits with breathless interest, whether hopefully or fearfully, for the results of the Marxist experiment in Russia.

## THE CONTEMPORARY CRISIS

This essay has been concerned with the historical background of the contemporary world on its inner side. It is not concerned to interpret the contemporary situation itself. All that remains to be said is this :

the clue that we have followed indicates with hardly
the possibility of a doubt that we are now in the throes
of another break-up in the cultural tradition, and at
the beginnings of a new stage in the advance of science
and of its application to the control of the conditions
of life. The inhibitions which hitherto have kept
science outside the field of human personality are
breaking down. Scientific psychology is developing.
Nature is fast disappearing as the central focus of
interest in the cultural field. Matter and the machine
are taking its place. What will be the outcome we
can only guess. But we should notice that when
culture has descended from God to matter it can
descend no farther, and that when science has successfully invaded the field of personality there is no other
field left for it to invade. It looks as though, when
the stage upon which we entered with the conclusion
of the War has run its course—and that course is likely
to be a rapid one—not merely will another stage in
the development of the European spirit be complete,
but the whole process which began at the end of the
Middle Ages will have fulfilled itself. As it reaches its
goal we can see that it is ceasing to be merely European
and becoming world-wide. The modern spirit, which
has been historically developed in the limited world of
European progress, is fast becoming the spirit of the
modern world. What is to follow we can hardly guess.
Almost certainly, a unified world civilization, based
upon the achievements of science. Perhaps also the
beginnings of a new culture which the modern spirit
will create for itself. For the spirit of man will starve
without culture, as surely as his body will starve without
food ; and the traditional culture, the capital which the
Middle Ages accumulated, and upon which the modern
spirit has nourished itself in its long effort to build
its factory and install its machinery, is almost spent.

## II

INTRODUCTORY

By JOHN MACMURRAY

MY business in this introductory chapter is to give you an idea of the scope of the symposium on 'Some Makers of the Modern Spirit,' and of the general purpose which lies behind it. On the surface the series consists of a set of biographical studies of nine great men who have left their mark on modern history. But there is more than the interest of reading about the lives of great men involved in the series. It is this something more which does not appear on the surface that I want to explain.

About a year ago the pressure of the economic crisis was just beginning to reveal its true character. We were all beginning to realize that it was not something momentary which would pass away and leave things much as they had been, but that a great effort of reconstruction would be necessary in which the greater part of the world would have to co-operate before the shadow could be lifted. One of the effects of the prolongation of the depression has been to concentrate all our minds upon the immediate problems of the present and to set us all wondering what is going to happen in the near future. The past year, if it has not brought us any nearer to a solution of our problem, has at least produced a very great change in our minds.

To a larger extent than we recognize we have adjusted ourselves to the changed conditions. It would be most interesting to discuss the changes that have come over our ways of thinking and our attitudes of mind during the past year, and I suggest it as a topic for discussion. But for the moment I merely wish to draw attention to the concentration on the present and the immediate future which it has made universal.

I draw your attention to this in order to explain the reason for thinking that the kind of study of the past which this book offers is of real importance at the present time. The future, the immediate future, which is growing rapidly out of the present state of affairs, is going to be very different from the past. We all know that in our bones, even when we try to persuade ourselves that it is not. We are opening a new chapter in European history, and it is one in which, as never before, we shall be called upon to make decisions of great difficulty and of far-reaching importance. It is no use any longer to wait for things to happen. It is no use to guess vaguely what will happen to us in the next ten or twenty years. The development of civilization has forced the control of events into our own hands. The future will be what we make it. I do not mean that we have an unlimited freedom of choice. But there are certain choices which we have to make. Our main difficulty, I believe, is to get quite clear what these choices are. Until we understand clearly the limitations of our position—and by that I mean what is really impossible —and also the freedom that we have within these limitations, we shall still be in a muddle.

Now, there is only one way to get clear about the possibilities in the immediate future, between which we are free to choose, and that is by understanding the present situation in which we find ourselves. If we can understand the present we shall be able, within limits, to forecast the future. But the present which we have to understand is a changing present. It is indeed a very rapid movement. To understand it we have to know where it has come from and how it has got to the point which it has now reached. The key to the future lies in the past. This is the first thing that I should like to emphasize. We are not concerned with the past merely from an interest in history for its own sake. We are concerned with the past as a clue to the present and the immediate future. Our aim is to throw light upon the modern world and its possibilities.

The second point to which I wish to draw attention is that the series is concerned with the inner side of the movement of the modern world—that is to say, with the development of the modern spirit. Ordinary history is mainly concerned with external events. It concentrates upon actions. But all human actions are the expressions of thoughts and feelings and purposes in people's minds, and that inner world of the spirit has a history of its own. What happens to a man in his lifetime no doubt depends a great deal upon external circumstances and material conditions over which he has little control. But it also depends upon himself, upon his thoughts and desires, upon his choices and his decisions. This is equally true of society. Different societies have different histories, partly because the conditions under which they live are different, but also partly because they have a different spirit, because they are swayed in their activities by different motives and by different ideas. This is, indeed, quite obvious, but we are apt to overlook its application. In the present crisis there are two factors which will determine our future. One is the external circumstances, geographical, economic, political and so on, in which we find ourselves.   It is this external situation which sets the limits to our freedom and determines what is possible for us and what is not.   The other is the modern spirit, by which I mean the ideas and motives and attitudes which determine the way we deal with our situation and in particular the desires and ideals which we seek to satisfy within the limits set for us by external circumstances.   It is this inner factor in the modern situation which these chapters are concerned with.   They are designed to help us to understand the movement of the modern spirit in our own day by understanding its history.   We shall be discussing where it came from and how it has come to be what it is in ourselves and our fellows.

All history is the story of changes in human life, and the history of the modern spirit is no exception to this rule.   But in external history the changes are fast and obvious.   Mind changes much more slowly and the changes are more difficult to detect and to define. One result of this is that the history of the inner life of a society needs to be considered over a long period of time to be understood.   The main ideas which have changed the mind of the world during the last six hundred years are very few in number.   They could probably be counted on the fingers of one hand.   In the history of political and social events it is a far cry to the Middle Ages.   But in the history of thought the Middle Ages is only yesterday.   If any one is inclined to think that this book, starting as it does from St. Thomas Aquinas and Martin Luther and coming down in the course of a few chapters to Karl Marx and Nietzsche, who are practically contemporary figures, has attempted to cover far too great a period of time, he should remember that it is only by taking such a sweep that we can see the modern spirit in its true perspective. Our minds are still largely dependent upon the medieval world, and the whole stretch of our history from Luther to the present economic crisis is a single chapter, and an incomplete chapter at that, in the inner history of human life. During that time one or two vigorous creative ideas have been born in our consciousness and have grown slowly to maturity. These one or two ideas lie behind the whole course of modern history and are working in our minds to-day to determine the new developments into which we are being forced so unceremoniously by the march of events. And these few ideas form the thread which binds us to the past and gives a human meaning to all that has happened to us in the last few centuries. In following these talks it is these few ideas that are important and it is for them that readers should be on the watch. The nine great men whose lives and activities will be discussed have all been chosen because they are associated in some vivid and significant way with the governing ideas which have shaped our history and at last, in their interrelation, formed the pattern of thought and action which we call the modern spirit.

Thomas Aquinas, who comes first on the list, stands as the representative of the medieval world from which the modern world has grown. In reading the chapter about him, one should try to use it to form a picture of the kind of world in which the modern spirit took its rise. He represents peculiarly well the medieval spirit at its best, and we must think of the medieval spirit not as something quite different and alien from our own, but rather as the stuff out of which the modern spirit has been made by the introduction of new ideas which have gradually transformed it. All the other men who appear in the series are moderns ; that is to say, they are representatives of the new ideas

D

which have worked the transformation. They fall naturally into three groups. In the first group I should put Luther, Rousseau, Goethe and Nietzsche as representatives of the great cultural ideas which have formed the modern spirit. I should have liked to call this group ' the men of religious ideas ' were it not for the fact that the term religion has been specialized in our ordinary speech so that only Luther would usually be recognized as a religious thinker. Yet the ideas which these men stand for are all religious in the sense that they concern the very heart of all human life, both individual and social, and so form our conception of the meaning and significance of life itself. In the second group I should put Newton and Darwin as the two most significant figures on the scientific side of the history of the modern spirit. The third group consists of Rousseau (on another side of his work), Bentham and Marx. This group represents the thinkers who have been effective in forming our conceptions of society and social organization. They stand in a sense intermediate between the other two groups, because our social ideas are concerned with giving effect, in the ordering of social, political and economic life, to the cultural or religious ideas which embody our sense of the significance of life. Our scientific ideas, on the other hand, provide us with the knowledge which enables us to control and use the forces of Nature for the supply of our needs and the accomplishment of our purposes. Social thinkers, therefore, bring together our scientific and our religious ideas by revealing how we must organize our social life if the power that science gives us is to be used to realize our ideals of what human life might be and ought to be.

Whether the purpose of the symposium as I have tried to state it for you is achieved or not will depend very largely upon the way you use the material that the different contributors provide. They have a difficult task because they are working within narrow limits of space. They have done what they can to suggest the connexions between the past and the present, and to relate the men they speak about and the ideas they stood for with our own time. But their efforts will be of no avail unless readers co-operate fully in the task. They can do this, in the first place, by getting a clear idea of the purpose of the series and keeping it in mind. This will keep them on the watch for the connexions which are suggested and for others which will suggest themselves. It would be well to keep asking at every point : ' What is the connexion of this man and his ideas with the present ? What is his significance for us now ? ' If readers do this, I believe that the rest will not be too difficult.

May I in closing say a word about the essay which forms the introduction to this book ? It tries to do what cannot be done, or only slightly, in the chapters themselves—to link together the different parts of the study by providing a clue to the history of the modern world on its inner side. It represents my own attempt to understand the modern situation by understanding how it has developed in men's minds through the past centuries. It is, of course, only one way of interpreting that history and a way with which many people will no doubt disagree. But in spite of that I hope that it will provide a frame of reference within which readers will be able to place the different men and ideas discussed in the rest of the book. Where they disagree I hope that it will help them to disagree clearly and to discover the reasons for their disagreement, and even to build up a different interpretation for themselves.

The gist of my own interpretation of the history of

the modern spirit I can put in a few words.  There are two and only two governing ideas which lie at the root of the development of the modern world.  The first is the idea of the freedom of the individual.  The second is the idea of the equality of all individuals.  The first was introduced into the traditional life of medieval Europe at the Reformation.  The second, which was added to it and did not take its place, arose with the French Revolution.  Alongside of these two ideas, and closely related to them, has gone the development of modern science.  Until a century ago the ideas of freedom and equality remained largely ideals which could not be fully realized in practice because human life was almost wholly at the mercy of Nature and under the control of economic conditions.  But with the development of science we began to discover how Nature could be controlled by human effort and subordinated to man.  It became possible to realize the ideals of freedom and equality in practical life.  To-day the world finds itself, so far as science is concerned, in a position to dominate Nature and so to realize the ideals which have governed our history, if we still wish to do so.  The idea of individual freedom has indeed been realized in the economic field to a large extent already.  Our industrial system is the result.  But the sister idea of equality has not.  Now democracy rests in idea upon the union of freedom and equality, so that the question facing the modern spirit at the present time, the question we must answer pretty soon in one way or another, is this :  ' Now that at last we have the power to do so, are we prepared to realize democracy, are we prepared to implement the promises of equal freedom in the practical field of economic life ? '

III

## ST. THOMAS AQUINAS

## (1225—1274)

### By The Rev. Father M. C. D'Arcy, S.J.

THE object of this symposium is, in the words of Professor Macmurray, ' to provide a background and a perspective for understanding the modern world,' and in the preceding chapter the changes which have taken place since the subject of my talk to-night, St. Thomas Aquinas, died in 1274, were described. Do not think that we are going an unnecessarily long way back or that the thirteenth century and medieval ideas are of little account. There are, I know, enthusiastic people who speak unguardedly as if they viewed everything that has happened in the last four hundred years as pernicious and wanted all of us to be thirteenth-century delving Adams and spinning Eves. That is silly, though notice that those of you who grow delirious about certain forms of modern art, calling it primitive, Egyptian, negro, and what not, are not in the position to sneer at others who prefer the medieval. If Gauguin and D. H. Lawrence in their different ways liked natives and savage forms, why should not a Pugin like his Gothic, Ruskin his Florentine and Venetian, Mr. Chesterton the social conditions of the Middle Ages

and I my St. Thomas Aquinas ?   I do, in fact, admire
him enormously, but I do not ask you to be so whole-
hearted.   It will be enough if you put aside prejudice
and make the attempt to realize how much you owe
to him.   He was separated in time far farther from
the Greeks than you are from him ; nevertheless he
took over what was best in Plato and Aristotle and
adapted it to the needs of his time.   There is no reason
why we should not do the same with his thought and
philosophy.

There were many other great thinkers and saints in
the Middle Ages besides St. Thomas, but wisely the
authors of this series have selected him, because he
epitomizes the life and thought of his time, and did
more than any other to give it shape.   In the thirteenth century the tidying process which had begun
after the great upheavals during the Dark Ages was in
full swing.   There was so much to do.   The Church
had been the one permanent institution when everything else fell into confusion.   Now that not only
family life but cities and ruling princes were able to
take stock of themselves a rapid process of development had set in.   There is no need for me to recall to
you the formation of what came to be called the Holy
Roman Empire.   You will find it all told admirably in
Mr. Dawson's book, *The Making of Europe*.   In St.
Thomas's lifetime an apparent completion of this
process of European unification was taking place, a
very striking concord, when all is said, of civilization
and culture under a dual authority, lay and spiritual.
This was a fulfilment of what had been dreamt of by
Plato in his optimistic years and is now, as we know
well, an imperative need.   In history books we read
more often of the conflicts between the popes and the
emperors, and this leads us to forget, as the late
Professor Tout wrote, ' the normal peaceful co-

operation of the ecclesiastical and the civil powers in the daily work of the medieval world.'

St. Thomas belonged to both powers. By blood he was related to Barbarossa and to the Kings of France, Castile and Aragon, and by choice he became a church-man, a humble friar in a new mendicant order. He was thus a man with many loyalties, who could imbibe the best in the Italian, German and French geniuses. From early youth, though he lived with a haughty father and brothers who loved fighting and foraging, he turned to study. This did not disturb his parents, who therefore planned an ecclesiastical career for him and thought the position of a territorial abbot might suit his rank and theirs. There was nothing small or ignoble in that, but providentially he went to the university at Naples to complete his studies, and there he came across a body of men called Friar-preachers. They were quite new and had been founded by one, Dominic, to meet the needs of the changing world.

Francis of Assisi and Dominic, twin spirits and re-formers, both play in their time a part similar to what Benedict had done when the Roman Empire collapsed, what Ignatius Loyola did, and, as some would say, Luther, at another critical moment of history, and what we should like to see done for us in some way at the present day. Francis wanted disciples who would be as simple and straightforward as the serf and the peasant and the folk without land, and at the same time he wished to fuse their spirit with the love of God and the virtues of the Sermon on the Mount. Thus the needs of the multitudes in the acquired lands and new cities of Europe could be met, and their lot be turned into one of happy contentment and holy perfection. Dominic, on the other hand, saw in the Albigensian heresy the menace of intellectual depravity, of false teaching and undisciplined thought in the youthful and headstrong students of the age, and his order had for object to foster the peace and unity of truth in this new civilization. Both orders were vowed to poverty, and their rule and ideal imposed on them a life of self-denial and heroism, as it was considered that no lasting remedial measures for society could be launched by men who shun self-sacrifice. The rich make poor preachers to the poor.

To this new order of the Friar-preachers St. Thomas was attracted, and the protests of his haughty family were of no effect. They, however, were not to be gainsaid, and when St. Thomas was sent to Cologne to study there, they waylaid him and carried him off a prisoner to his own home. All sorts of efforts were made to weaken his resolution ; they even made attempts on his virtue, but on this one occasion the young man, now grown to a great height and strength, flew into such a passion of indignation that they did not try again. Instead, they at length permitted him to escape ; they couldn't stop him praying and thinking and he was imperceptibly making them, too, holy. So Thomas got finally to Cologne and sat at the feet of the most celebrated thinker of his day, Albert the Great. It was while there he gained the nickname of the ' dumb ox ' ; he seems to have said little and thought much. Albert, however, recognized his genius and, as I shall explain in a moment, made him his companion in the revolution of thought he was contemplating. He also saw that he should go to Paris, then the centre of the intellectual activities of Europe. Arrived there he took the degree of master in theology at the age of thirty-one and began to teach. From the first his lectures attracted attention for what one of his con-temporaries has described as a ' new method, new arguments, new points of doctrine, new order of questions, new light.' He clearly did not seek publicity. There is a charming letter of his of advice to a young student which reveals his own habits :

' Since you have asked me in Christ, dear John, to tell you how you must study to attain a treasury of knowledge, I shall mention the following points of advice ; and amongst these are the following : Be chary of speech ; take great heed of the purity of your conscience ; love to be diligent in your cell, if you would be led to the wine cellar of wisdom. Ever be loving towards all ; do not bother yourself about the doings of others. Don't gad about ; consider not from whom you hear anything, but fix in your mind everything good that is said ; make an effort thoroughly to understand whatever you read and hear. In all doubt seek to penetrate to the truth.'

Nevertheless it was impossible for him to be hid. Paris was a cauldron ever bubbling over with the excitement of new ideas. Our modern universities descend from the great experiments in education at this period. During the Dark Ages the bishops and monasteries had managed to preserve some of the great literature of Greece and Rome, pagan and Christian, and they had not let the tradition of learning die out. By their means and with the authority of Charlemagne schools were started where sufficiently peaceful conditions allowed, and from these the universities developed. A great teacher gathered pupils around him, and as Paris had been very lucky in its teachers it went ahead of the others. By the time of St. Thomas students rich and poor and of many countries flocked to it. Gathered under masters, in a kind of guild, they would sit on straw mats listening for hours to the arguments propounded by the lecturer. They were

quarrelsome, very youthful, and being without newspapers or wireless or shockers, their interest lay in the
arts and philosophy instead of murder cases and foot-
ball results.   In order to understand the influence of
St. Thomas we must stop for a moment to consider the
main issues of the time.  Just as now, there were
then conservatives of the die-in-the-ditch type who were
affronted by the whirlwind energy of youth and the
swift development of thought on social and intellectual
matters.    There existed, too, dialecticians and sophists
and revolutionaries who gave legitimate cause for
anxiety.  Life, perhaps, was too uncomfortable, too
austere, to invite theories of pleasure, though the
songs of the period ring at times with pagan gusto and
bluff sensualism.   But if luxury was not thought of,
intemperance and social anarchy were real dangers.
Moreover, the great questions of the relation of Church
to State, of faith to reason, of the rights of man and
the adjustment of his earthly duties and hopes with
the unworldliness demanded of him as a Christian and
pilgrim of eternity, had to be settled.   To solve the
problem of faith and reason some Arabian thinkers
had invented the theory of a double truth, one for
religion and one for reason, what now we would call
religious experience and science, and agreement between them was not required.   In general it may be
said that Europe had reached a stage in which it had
to take stock of its past and prepare for the future of its
culture and civilization.

The early Christian Church had, as the distinguished
German scholar, Troeltsch, has pointed out, bequeathed the problem of its relation to the Greek and
Roman civilization without answering it.   Its own past
was Jewish and Oriental, and the Jewish culture, while
retaining a specific theological character of its own, was
rich with all the splendour of the Orient.   The in-

habitants of Egypt and Babylon, of Persia and Asia Minor, contributed to the formation of the people of Israel, and Christianity, though, in its Founder and in His teaching, it gave something entirely new to the world, was steeped in the wisdom from which it withdrew itself. Now the Empire in which it had to grow turned for its intellectual life to the Greeks. Their unparalleled fertility in thought seemed almost to have exhausted the powers of man in his search for truth, and even now we cannot escape the influence of Plato and Aristotle, the Stoics and the Epicureans. The schools of the first two are as vigorous as ever to-day, and leading scientists fit their new theories into their schemata, while all of us at times catch ourselves bowing to what can only be called the Stoic and Epicurean faith. What was wanting in the Greek genius the Roman supplied, namely, a calm, conscientious and clear-sighted discipline, the straight, persevering roads, the legal codes in which moral ideals are made definite and practical. Yet to the Christian all this magnificent expression of energy was pagan, and the pagan would not yield an inch in his pride or countenance what he deemed sheer fanaticism and anarchical. By the fourth century a compromise had been effected and the scene was staged for a proper reconciliation ; but the fall of the Empire destroyed all immediate hopes, and it was not until the thirteenth century that the opportunity arrived again, and this time on a still grander scale. Christianity had triumphed. Instead of being an outlaw, it had to make law, to lay down the natural law which would define the rights and duties and happiness of man, the laws governing families and states and society, the laws too which should prove themselves to be the fundamental principles underlying all Nature and all existences from the highest to the lowest ; and there before it lay all the wisdom of the Greeks, the Hebrews and the East on the one side, and a Christian but wild youth on the other.

To the Church must be given the credit of dressing ' into a dexterous and starlight order ' all this jostling and apparently ill-assorted company, social, intellectual and religious, of combining history with thought, and so making Christianity the one intellectual religion which is also historical ; but the chief agent in the transformation was undoubtedly St. Thomas Aquinas. He began by making a revolutionary change in two important matters of debate. Up to his time all the preference of the chief thinkers had been for Plato or rather Platonism. The higher reaches of Plato's thought fitted the Christian theology, and from the time of Augustine in the West and earlier in the East, Platonism had dominated. Aristotle indeed was known, but chiefly as a logician, for the works of his which survived were his logical treatises. His greater works came at first to Paris through the Arabians, and the Arabians interpreted him in a manner ir-reconcilable at times with Christian theology. St. Thomas and Albert the Great observed with dismay this false, as they thought, interpretation ; they studied Aristotle afresh, had correct translations made of his major works, which were now available, and with his help St. Thomas propounded a new synthesis of philosophy which was more universal and more logically coherent and systematic than any one which had been hitherto conceived. The weakness of Christian Platonism lay in this, that it neglected the lowest levels of life ; the material and the sensible are only half real—shadows not substantial things ; the home of the spirit is away from such things, and the soul imprisoned in the body longs for release to abide where absolute truth and beauty dwell. If a rough generalization may be permitted, Platonism in history, I do not say Plato, corresponds with a perennial tendency in man ; it marks his dissatisfaction with the temporal, with the passing shows of this life and the limitations of body and sense.  It is difficult with this philosophy and this outlook to justify the pleasures of the senses, marriage and feasting, and the labours and joys which Mother Earth provides.  St. Thomas did not let go the element of truth in this tendency, but with astonishing vigour and sureness of touch he brought into an alliance with it a philosophy which gave full value to the body, which declared that man was only fully man when he was body as well as soul ; he allowed for all the modern discoveries of the intimate connexion of the physical and the physiological with the psychical ; he gave honour to all God's creatures, and by thus raising the dignity of physical nature, of the body, of natural virtue and natural pursuits, of human rights and human duties, he may be said to have emancipated Nature and man, and given them over to future generations to study and love.

The second change he made is closely connected with this, as it concerns the relation of faith to reason.  The truth he enunciated was part of Christian belief from the beginning, but as faith was concerned with the most sacred of treasure, the Word spoken from on high and made flesh, and as assistance from God was necessary in order to be able to see and bear in mind the new way of the revelation of the new way of life into the secrets of the Godhead, it was natural that many should extol faith at the expense of reason and suspect the latter's efficacy when applied curiously and vauntingly to what was above it.  St. Thomas scandalized some of his contemporaries by his vindication of the rights of reason and his clear division of natural philosophy and science where reason was dominant, the judge, and supernatural religion where authority was the first source. Throughout his life he sought truth and truth in its purity. 'If a man departs from truth he is void of understanding,' he declared. In his humility he was quite content to give the credit to past philosophers when he thought they had made real discoveries, and he seems at times to be a mere echo of Aristotle. But this is an illusion. He was free from any party ; he swore by no master save truth itself, and so it is no surprise to find a modern thinker like Professor Whitehead saying that the most rationalist period of history was the medieval. To St. Thomas we owe in part that charta of liberty which established science, and the clear demarcation of the spheres of authoritative Christian religion and natural philosophy.

The working out of his views occupied all the spare moments of his short life. Possessed of a memory that never forgot and unswerving concentration, he wrote in the forty-eight years of his life what ten now could scarcely accomplish. We know something of his habits, that he spent part of the night in prayer, and kept strictly to the rules and customs of his order. He had no taste for pomp or popularity ; he was simple and ingenuous, most tender and charming to friends, and ever ready to sacrifice himself for them. So highly did his order and the Papacy think of him that they several times summoned him to their aid when difficult decisions had to be taken and wise counsel was needed. St. Thomas gave all the help he could, and begged all the same to be allowed to remain a simple friar instead of being elevated to a bishopric. These duties took him away from Paris for a time, but his writing went on uninterruptedly. His greatest masterpiece, the *Summa Theologica*, was nearly finished when he died at the early age of forty-eight. He had worn himself out, and his love of God had become such a consuming passion that his pen refused to write. When his beloved companion, Reginald, implored him to go on, he replied : ' I can no more ; such things have been revealed to me that what I have written seems but straw.'

No doubt his unremitting energy and the opposition he had to face had helped to sap his strength. The last years of his life had been spent in conflict. After he had left Paris a strong party of opposition had gathered strength there ; conservatives and extremists joined hands to wreck his work, and so he had to come back in haste in 1268. For once we feel in his writings the presence of passion and just indignation. ' If then any one there be who, boastfully taking pride in his supposed wisdom, wishes to challenge what we have written, let him not do it in some corner nor before children who are powerless to decide on such difficult questions. Let him reply openly if he dare. He shall find me there confronting him, and not only my negligible self, but many another whose interest is truth. We shall do battle with his errors or bring a cure to his ignorance.' For days he had to stand every kind of attack publicly in the staged argumentative trials which the medieval students loved. His opponents were rude to him, and lost their tempers while the saint, quiet and controlled, without rebuke or recrimination, crushed the objections to powder. His victory was so complete that it became a favourite subject of art and is represented in works at Florence, Pisa, Paris and in the Church of S. Maria sopra Minerva in Rome. His object attained, as he thought, St. Thomas left Paris in order, at the request of Charles of Anjou, to reorganize studies in Naples, and in 1274 he set out to attend a council at Lyons, accompanied by his dearest companion, Reginald. He stopped on the way to see his sister and there became so weak that he was given the last sacraments of the Church. On receiving his viaticum he was overcome with emotion and cried out : ' I receive Thee, ransom of my soul. For love of Thee have I studied and taught and kept vigil, toiled, preached and taught. Never have I said a word against Thee.' These words give a fitting end to one who had written some of the most stately and beautiful hymns in Christendom in honour of Corpus Christi, and had become wise and saintly through his love and knowledge of God.

In summarizing his contribution to mankind it is difficult to know where to begin and where to end. As you probably know well, a large part of Christendom, scattered throughout the world and numbering amongst them many of the finest intellects of their day, have taken him as ' the master of all that know ' from his death, down to our own time. The *Divina Commedia* of Dante rose from his ashes ; he was the inspiration of that great band of mystics which included Ruysbroek, Tauler and Suso ; his writings became the text-book of Europe and the chief authority in every university. At the present time there are flourishing schools of Thomism in Germany, France, Italy, Belgium and the United States ; several contemporary statesmen have studied and sought to apply his principles to their national problems, and if we seek for a body of well-defined and coherent doctrines, for a disciplined teaching and world-view to set alongside the teaching of social theories of dialectical materialism, it is almost inevitable that we should turn to St. Thomas. One reason why this is so I have already suggested. He stands at a point of history from which he is able to gather up all the riches of the past and give the keyword for the future. But this reason is not enough. A philosopher is said to be able to look

before and after ; he must also look up and down, and
make a ladder between heaven and earth. Whereas
so many thinkers and reformers grope falteringly,
have flashes of insight and long stretches of darkness,
or spend themselves watering some tiny garden of the
universe, St. Thomas gives the impression of knowing
the movement and direction of the universe and man,
as though he had climbed to some vantage spot where-
from he could see the final end and so trace both from
the beginning and from the terminus the nature and
destiny of human life. Hence all falls into order in
his philosophy and in the graph he draws he is able to
mark out the place and function of man. Of course
an infinite number of facts and truths have been discovered since his time, and there is room for difference
on many of his arguments, but the background remains. For those of us who admit a God, it seems that
St. Thomas saw deeper into the mind of God than
any other thinker and interpreted faithfully and wisely
the plan and purposes of Him who made all things, and
even those of you who are slow to believe must admit
that we are as likely to destroy as benefit a work of art,
a living thing and above all man himself if we have
no true idea of what it or he is *for*.

In order then to show more concretely the contribution which St. Thomas has made, I will end by developing a little his conception of man or human nature,
and just mention some of the other things he did. He
gave to religious philosophers the rational grounds for
a belief in God in the famous five proofs, which I
think still defy criticism : he gave the solution to the
problem which defeated the Indian philosophers and
so vexed the Western, how God can be infinitely distinct
from us and yet knowable by us, or to put it in another
way, how we can be distinct from God, relatively
independent units, and yet belong to Him most utterly :

E

he supplied the arguments for the possibility of a supernatural order and God's intercourse with man in the Christian revelation : he showed that religion could and should be reasonable, and laid down the lines on which a Christian State could be realized ; he divined the intimate connexion of love and knowing, desire and reason in human conduct and activities, anticipating here, if I may say so, and supplementing whatever truth there is in psycho-analysis and the new psychology, and finally, so as not to go on too long with this list, he worked out the relations of religion, philosophy and the physical sciences in a way which guarantees true science, and would save many of its exponents from going beyond their brief, if they would but read his pages.

But it is in his teaching about human nature that he perhaps most of all excels, and has a message for our own day.  Man is the meeting-place of two worlds, the material and the spiritual.  He is cousin to the animals, and like them he is determined in part by inheritance and environment, by instincts and changing moods and tenses, by physical and economic factors. But as having a mind he is also self-reflective, can escape the wheel of necessity, and by thought standing above himself can control and direct his own life, according to the vision of absolute and unchanging beauty and truth which that mind unrolls before him.  True indeed, that he is not entirely free, that he is sense-bound, that he is happiest when the abstract thoughts are clothed in flesh and blood, and confirmed by sensible experience.  Nevertheless any philosophy which would declare man to be nothing more than a superior animal, or on the other hand a mind and nothing else, is false to the facts.  Man is both, and that is his secret, the ground of his infirmity and struggling lot, and also of his dignity.  If in many regards he

comes so near to the animal he is by mind near to
God, an active reflection of the universe, and a person
with rights and duties. From this conception of
human nature St. Thomas proceeds with firm and
bold strokes to outline the ideal which can be realized
on this earth and the immortal destiny of man, and
to define his rights to property, his duties in society,
sovereignty and the best forms of government. Law,
as you know, ranked very high in the minds of medieval
thinkers, and St. Louis, for example, King of France
and friend of St. Thomas, surrendered to the English
Crown districts which had fallen to the French because
he could not be convinced of his right to retain them.
And the reason for this respect is given by St. Thomas
when he argues from the nature of man that there
must be a law set within man's nature by God and
experienced in conscience which directs him to his
proper perfection, and that the first precepts of this
law are the foundation of community life. As family
and social life are essential for the welfare of man,
they are said to be founded on natural law, and an
attempt even was made to bring the interrelations of
peoples and races within the moral order, and to
make all human pursuits and all dealings of men
with men moral and holy.

The sacred character of justice and the respect paid
to law, and indeed many of the customs which still
survive in England, owe their origin to the beliefs
which St. Thomas welded together in his vast *Summa*.
Other ideas, which you will hear of in later lectures,
were mingled with those which after twelve centuries
of growth came to a head in the thirteenth century,
so that now they linger on in manners and in sentiment
without any knowledge of their intellectual justification.
Whereas a disciple of St. Thomas could write that ' the
object of gain is that by means of it man may provide

for himself and others according to their state. The object of providing for himself and others is that they may be able to live virtuously. The object of a virtuous life is the attainment of everlasting glory,' and whereas St. Thomas made man a very minor royalty under the supreme dominion of God, with the noble faculty of free will to choose the right and do good, the modern world has been governed by the thought of one who said that liberty was an end in itself and the most sacred of privileges. By that saying the State became the supreme arbiter of morals instead of the guardian, and an unrestricted freedom to compete and struggle took on the aspect of a virtue. The change is well worth noting. St. Thomas thought that man by his very nature as the lowest of spiritual creatures should have his mind and will educated and disciplined to perfection and then be allowed to exercise his freedom in social life and heighten his personality by the rights and duties of ownership. The later theory said that liberty was inviolable, and so the State left man to think and desire what he liked, and occupied itself with interfering with his home life and material needs and mulcting him of his possessions ; and as this has led to the misery we see all round us, another theory has come to the fore, which, not content with depriving man of his right to personal goods, wishes to subject to its own deterministic theory his liberty also of mind and will. I think we might well reconsider, as so many social writers are asking us to do, the views of St. Thomas on this vital matter and see whether we may not profit by them.

I shall have performed my task, therefore, if I ask you to look back on the world in which St. Thomas lived, and to reflect, in the light of modern problems and our contemporary civilization, on the ideals he embraced. Man is the centre of the visible universe.

The world they knew then was small as compared
with ours in size, and we are far less clear of his privileged position. But we must remember that if in
size the world was small, in stretch theirs was far
larger, for the life of man was held with absolute
certainty to reach into eternity, and instead of galaxies
of stars they believed in real and possible worlds of
varying orders and spirits and the far-off splendour of
a real God of infinite goodness. No matter how many
physical worlds there may prove to be they are subject
to the understanding of man, and he can grasp them
in the unity of his mind and adapt them to the purposes
of his soul. Man again has a clear purpose. St.
Thomas saw all things co-ordinated to their last end,
and man surrounded by the Providence of God with
a definite object to attain and a definite work to do.
The Christian religion had lifted the mists which gather
round the peaks of thought, and since man found truth
by sensible experience, the Word of God had mani-
fested itself to man through the sensible and the
concrete. The Incarnation is to religious thought
what empirical investigation is to science, and the
Church of the thirteenth century strove to combine
with human society after the manner of the Word
which became flesh. Thus the vision of a unified
world, a Christian commonwealth, came close to
fulfilment, and Europe has been haunted by that
vision ever since. In the Middle Ages the principle
of unity was spiritual, and whereas the modern
world has sought for that unity by science or economics,
our ancestors held that science and economics were
lower than man, and that man was lower than God,
and that unity could be consummated only by the
highest factor. The Christian religion rallied the
people into ranks, each with a purpose and function,
each protected by guilds, by a common moral code

and sanctions. The spiritual power had to be the servant of the servants of God ; the religious orders had to practise a voluntary communism that they might be more free for contemplative wisdom or the service of their fellows ; the temporal sovereign had to rule by moral law, and his right to command rested on a moral authority conferred on him by God to be used for the welfare of his subjects. The lot of man was hard; that was his own fault because he freely acknowledged the fact of sin, but it was lit up by a felicitous providence and by faith and hope in the Incarnation and a time to come when all tears should be washed away. And lastly the way to the unseen kingdom of divine loveliness was charted out by dogma. To many of you dogma may appear as a restriction on liberty of thought. There you differ from the medieval ; St. Thomas would have said that it is no blessing to be set down in a jungle in the name of liberty, and that it is better far to be given a map to the land of promise and plenty with the power to choose the highest.

Be that as it may, there is the picture of the past, in rosy colours, no doubt, but true in essentials, and it is good to study our modern problems in the light of it. We all want happiness for others and ourselves. If you wish for a word of wisdom from St. Thomas as to how to obtain it, I cannot do better than quote and end with one remark of his. ' The sufficiency of corporal goods,' he says, ' and of the life of virtue is the end of human confederation ; but since the life of virtue is itself ordained to something infinitely higher— namely, the blessed Vision of God—this ultimate purpose of individual human life must be also the ultimate purpose of any human confederation. The end of the State, therefore, is the Vision of God.'

IV

## LUTHER

(1483—1546)

By The Rev. NATHANIEL MICKLEM, M.A., D.D.

*Principal and Professor of Dogmatic Theology, Mansfield
College, Oxford*

THERE are enthusiastic Protestants who ascribe
to Dr. Martin Luther, the saint and hero of
Wittenberg, all the liberties we enjoy, all the triumphs
of the modern spirit in science, literature, art and
statecraft, all that is free in our religion, all that
is liberal in our civilization. There are fervid Catholics
on the other side who look back to Luther as the
renegade monk whose recklessness and folly, headstrong
violence and self-will, issued in the rise of capitalism
and the evils that beset our economic order, in the
nationalism and moral anarchy that caused the War
and have prevented any durable and lasting peace,
in religious anarchy, in rationalism, subjectivism,
atheism, and a secular and godless civilization.

Exaggerated and even hysterical as these views may
be, neither is altogether without justification. Since
religion is one of the strongest forces in human life, it
is not surprising that the great religious controversy
and schism which was the prelude to the modern

world should to this day affect almost every aspect of our many-sided civilization. Luther, whether for praise or blame, was a man of astonishing natural force and vitality, a daemonic figure, explosive and dynamic, such a man as, if he find the ground prepared for him, is bound to set his stamp upon an epoch. . . .

Luther is of those who are either greatly loved or greatly hated. I hope I am not blind to his defects. I cannot offer him the reverential respect that I have for St. Thomas Aquinas, or the almost affectionate esteem with which I regard Erasmus ; but there is a personal greatness about Luther, an elemental force, an evangelical passion, which make it natural to class him with St. Augustine and St. Paul.[1] He made great mistakes, was guilty of astonishing inconsistencies, and was certainly no immaculate stained-glass-window saint ; but a saint I think he was in the evangelical sense and a great Christian ; for better, for worse, he was undoubtedly one of the ' makers of the modern spirit.'

First I admire him as a man of splendid and indomitable courage, both physical and moral. He feared the face of no man ; taking his life in his hand and disregarding the anxious warnings of all his friends, he would go to Worms to face the Emperor, though there were as many devils there as there were tiles upon the roof. ' We are coming, my Spalatin,' he writes, ' although Satan has tried to stop me with more than one sickness. The whole way from Eisenach here I have been miserable, and am still in a way not before experienced. Charles's mandate, I know, has been

---

[1] The most balanced and adequate judgement upon Luther known to me is Professor Heiler's article entitled *Luther's Bedeutung für die christliche Kirche* in the volume *Luther in ökumenischer Sicht.* 1929. For a modern scientific critical estimate of Luther (by a Protestant) see Böhme's *Luther and the Reformation in the Light of Modern Research.* Eng. Tr. 1930. See also Holl, *Gesammelte Aufsätze.* Vol. I.

published to frighten me. But Christ lives, and we will enter Worms in spite of all the gates of hell and powers of the air.' ' What ! ' said a cardinal to him on one occasion. ' Do you think the Pope cares for the opinion of a German boor ? The Pope's little finger is stronger than all Germany. Do you expect your princes to take up arms to defend you—you, a wretched worm like you ? I tell you, No ! and where will you be then—where will you be then ? ' ' Then as now,' answered Luther, ' in the hands of Almighty God.'

Hence there is about him an abandon, a gaiety, almost a boyish irresponsibility. He walked with something of the soldier's gait. ' He leaned backward rather than forward,' we are told. ' His eyes sparkle and glitter like a star,' says one who saw him, ' so that it is hardly possible to look at them.' He was utterly carefree, illimitably generous ; he lived from day to day and recked little of consequences. ' There is a marvellous overflowing freedom from care,' says von Schubert, ' in this Luther, which in spite of all differences forcibly reminds us of Francis.'[1] But, as von Schubert points out, the Italian saint lacked the sovereign gift of humour which enabled Luther to enter into the life of the world and yet to laugh at it and its weaknesses, because his soul was ever in the sunshine of a sure trust in the Heavenly Father : ' God is pleased to allure us that we may believe He is our true Father, and we are His true children.'

Luther's humour was very pithy, often boisterous, and sometimes astonishingly coarse ; he never hesitated to put the thumb of ridicule to the nose of contempt. His conduct must often seem scandalous to those who connect sanctity with discipline and decorum and the virtues of restraint. He must have been astonishingly free from what we call inhibitions and morbid

[1] *Grosse christliche Personlichkeiten*, p. 141.

complexes.   Never in any degree did he play the saint.
Flowers he loved, and music and children ; and when
they asked him : ' Where will you bide if the ban of
the Church fall upon you ? ' he answered : ' Under the
sky.'

I certainly do not hold up Luther as a model of all
Christian virtues, but he has been most vilely traduced
in the course of controversy.   If you have been led to
doubt whether at heart he was a good man and a
Christian man, you should read Böhme's careful
sifting of the evidence.   I feel disposed to say that if
ever a man lived as a child of God, it was Luther—a
very high-spirited child, a very headstrong child, a
very naughty child only too often, but with an extraordinary directness, an extraordinary unself-conscious-
ness, an extraordinary abandon. . . .

From the point of view of the Church of Rome he
is, of course, a heretic.   But, as Heiler rightly points
out, he is a heretic of an almost unique kind.   He is a
heretic because he rediscovered, and was seized by,
one cardinal element in the faith of Catholic Christianity which had been so overlaid as to be virtually
forgotten, and he proclaimed it to the exclusion of
all else.   Protestants who rejoice at the Reformation
must remember that the schism was a tragedy whose
sad fruits were never more apparent than to-day, and
Roman Catholics may well reflect that had the Roman
Church reformed itself before Luther's day, as it did
soon afterwards, there might well have been no schism.

Luther's religious position might, I think, be summed
up in untechnical terms as the discovery of freedom.
He himself might put it in this way, that the Lord
Christ has triumphed over the devil and over sin, over
death and over the Law, and that man by faith in
Christ may enjoy all the benefits of His victory.

In the reality of the devil and of evil spirits round

about us, in the dreadful efficacy of sorcery and witch-
craft, Luther believed not less strongly than all his
contemporaries. From terror he had come to peace.

> And were this world all devils o'er,
>   And watching to devour us,
> We lay it not to heart so sore ;
>   Not they can overpower us.
>     And let the prince of ill
>     Look grim as e'er he will,
>     He harms us not a whit ;
>     For why ?  His doom is writ ;
> A word shall quickly slay him.

Waking up in the night, conscious that Satan himself,
the powerful prince of darkness, was in the room, he
could say to him : ' Oh, it's only you, is it ? ' and fall
asleep again. Christ had defeated Satan.

Luther had a far deeper sense of sin and moral im-
potence than most of his contemporaries. If labours,
fastings, penances and ascetic discipline could make a
man good, there was no height of goodness to which
he would not have forced his way ; but all his struggles
and prayers brought him no peace, till it came to him
that Christ loved sinners, that it was sinners whom he
came to save, for Christ has triumphed over sin.

Over all that medieval world there hung the shadow
of death, and after death the Judgement. Luther was
utterly delivered from this dread. He did not seek
martyrdom ; he took a very healthy and natural
pleasure in the good things of life that came his way
(though for himself he lived sparingly and simply) ;
but like Johann Sebastian Bach he looked upon death
as an angel, a minister of God, and not an enemy.
Sinner that he knew himself to be, he trusted his soul
to Christ and was persuaded that He was able to keep

that which was committed to Him. Christ had triumphed over death.

Christ had even triumphed over conscience. Luther, it may be freely admitted, was not the proper subject for the monastic life. Such a man in the modern Roman Church would doubtless be told that he had no vocation for it. The life as a monk may have accentuated an almost morbid, moral hypersensitiveness in him. His wise director, Johann von Staupitz, thought there was something abnormal in his sense of sin. Yet whatever Luther's superiors and companions might say to comfort him, his conscience remained burdened, and he could find no peace. Peace and illumination came to him as he pondered the passage in the epistle to the Romans i. 17: 'Therein is revealed a righteousness of God from faith unto faith, as it is written. But the righteous shall live by faith.' Righteousness is not man's attainment but God's gift. Christ had triumphed even over conscience.

Hence the freedom, the abandon, the gaiety, the assurance of Luther. He displayed many of the qualities (may I be forgiven for saying this !) whereby Mr. G. K. Chesterton has so endeared himself to the Christian public—but in a more eminent degree. He was like a bird escaped from the fowler's net, and it was typical of him that when the citizens of Wittenberg followed him with their plaudits, ' Luther for ever ! ' he answered : ' Nay, Christ for ever ! '

This is the man who as much as any may be said to have turned the course of history, and to have been a ' maker of the modern spirit.' Let us consider his influence for later times—(a) political, (b) economic, (c) national. . . .

(a) When we turn to the economic and political life of the modern world and to modern civilization as

a whole, it is clearly impossible to disentangle and
analyse the various elements in the vast complex so
as to ascribe to Luther with any definiteness his due
place in the whole. I at any rate am quite incompetent
for so delicate and exacting a task. I take it, however,
that this is not required of me. For the purposes of
this series Luther stands for the influence upon the
modern spirit of that Protestantism of which he was
the protagonist and in some sense the founder. There
can be no question that Protestantism is one of the
formative influences of the modern world, and I shall
satisfy the needs of this occasion (though not of exact
scholarship) if I try to indicate what the modern spirit
owes to the Protestant movement.

Both the Jesuit Fr. Grisar and the Protestant von
Harnack agree that Luther is not in any exact sense to
be called the creator of the modern spirit.[1] Troeltsch
is justified in the opinion that Luther belongs rather
to the medieval world than to the modern.[2] ' The
Reformation,' says a witty writer, ' was confessedly an
attempt to solve a problem in subtraction rather than
in addition.'[3] Indeed, a very strong case could be
made out for the view that the modern world does not
begin with the Reformation at all or the Renaissance,
but with that critical and rationalistic movement of
the seventeenth and eighteenth centuries which is
often called the Illumination or Aufklärung. Certain
it is that Luther, could he revisit the earth to-day, would
be immeasurably astonished to be told that he was in
any way responsible for that situation which the newspapers describe to us, and he might well find it difficult
even to recognize modern Protestantism as any child
of his.

[1] *Luther*, by Hartmann Grisar, Vol. I, p. 387.
[2] *Protestantism and Progress*, pp. 59f. cf. pp. 85f.
[3] *The Unrealists*, by Harvey Wickham, p. 76.

Yet, if we cannot isolate the influence of Luther to-day, we can clearly detect it.  Freedom is apt to be a heady wine, and those who have found freedom in one sphere of life will be likely to demand it in all others.  ' A large section of the people of Germany,' says Professor Grant,[1] ' came to believe that under the guidance of Luther they had attained to a knowledge of the pure truth, which had so long been hidden beneath the corruptions and superstitions of the Catholic Church ; that, if this truth were preached abroad, all the world would accept it, and that it could only be resisted by stupidity or greed.  So there arose in Germany that vision of a better future, in religion, in politics, and in social life, which is the greatest of revolutionary forces.'  Thus the German Reformation actually had political consequences which Luther himself neither foresaw nor desired.

Luther had nothing of the political democrat in him, but the connexion between the Reformation movement and modern democracy is intimate.  The connexion, briefly stated, is this : the Reformation in England issued partly in the Elizabethan religious settlement, and partly in Independency (or, as it is now called in its modern dress, Congregationalism) ; it was the Independents who sailed for America in the *Mayflower*, and whose principles so greatly coloured the political ideas of North America.  Broadly, the Reformation produced the Pilgrim Fathers, and the Pilgrim Fathers inspired modern political democracy.  Such a statement is a gross over-simplification of the facts and seems like a slight to France, but it indicates a very important historical link. . . .

The earliest colonial democracy, however, was really a new form of *theocracy*.  The new colony must, of course, be ruled by God, and God's rule will be

[1] *A History of Europe*, p. 484.

exercised through magistrates popularly appointed in
virtue of their gifts for ruling in the fear of God.   There
is nothing here of ' the voice of the people the voice of
God,' of the inalienable political ' rights of man,' of
' majority rule,' of one man being as good as another,
of the clap-trap of modern democratic rhetoricians.
While, therefore, Protestantism is one of the parents
of modern democracy, it would manifestly be unfair
that Protestantism should get all the praise (or is it
blame ?) for democracy as it has developed in Europe
and America.   Still, as Principal Lindsay said : ¹' The
message which spoke of a religious democracy could
not fail to suggest the social democracy also.'

But we might come at the matter from another angle.
Luther's Reformation was on one side a great assertion
of human freedom, of the spiritual worth and dignity
of the common man, of the rights of private judgement.
Hence, it is said, arises that individualism which is
so predominant a mark of the modern spirit and which,
on its political side, is represented by modern demo-
cracies.   It is difficult here to adjust responsibility.
There can be no doubt that individualism, subjectivism
and the repudiation of authority are very distinctive
marks of the modern spirit, but how far they issue
from Protestantism cannot easily be determined.   My
impression is that classical Protestantism contributed
here unconsciously or even against its will to a movement
which really arose from other sources and had little
real affinity with it. . . .

Luther himself was no democrat, no patron of the
freedom of scientific inquiry ; he was the relentless
enemy of lawlessness, of sectaries, of those who pre-
tended some special inner light and private inspiration ;
yet because men who had found freedom in the sphere
of religion were persons of character and force, and

¹ *Encyclopaedia Britannica*, ed. XI, p. 138.

powerfully attracted to freedom everywhere, the Protestant movement undoubtedly proved one of the great creative forces of the modern world, taking up into itself elements originally alien to it and sometimes incompatible with its own inner logic.

(b) We have seen the close, but indirect, connexion between Luther and modern political democracy; we have now to consider the industrial or economic order. The modern world is distinguished from the medieval by the rise of capitalism. There is something grotesque in the suggestion that Luther is the father of modern capitalism; yet there seems to be no doubt that there is a very close connexion between Protestantism and capitalism. . . .

In Luther's day the spirit of heroism, of devotion, of sacrifice, found its expression and fulfilment in the cloister. Men were willing to renounce the world in the hope of gaining a heavenly treasure. He turned men's minds away from the monastery to find their divine vocation in the ordinary world. His most mighty successor was John Calvin, who not only set aside the old canon-law prohibition of interest and abolished many medieval restrictions on investment, but still more important, produced by his doctrine and discipline a new type of Christian piety, rugged, determined, self-reliant and ascetic, the type familiar to us in the Puritans of England and the Covenanters of Scotland. Such men sought the glory of God by strenuous and disciplined living in life's ordinary vocations. When in the course of time the religious impulse weakened, the mentality remained, and concerning itself solely with this world may be called ' the capitalistic spirit.' Capitalism is thus the child of Calvinistic Protestantism, a child that has repudiated its parent's faith. Luther turned men's minds from the monastic ideal and bade them find in civil occu-

pations the direct service of God ; Calvin taught men
to redress the world to the glory of God ; capitalism
has inspired men to subdue the world by labour and
discipline to the earthly advantage of the fortunate
and strong.

(c) It is widely recognized that one of the chief evils
under which the modern world is groaning is an
excessive and intolerant nationalism. May we, as
some suppose, ascribe the origin of this trouble also to
poor Martin Luther ? There can be no doubt that
the rise of a fierce nationalism is largely contempora-
neous with the Reformation, and that Luther is only
less a national than a religious hero. Even at the
Diet of Worms it was his conscious hope ' to do some
service to my Germany.'

The Middle Ages saw some genuine internationalism
in Europe, something like a common European civilization under the rule of Christ represented by His Church.
It is natural to contrast this happy state with the
divisions, bitternesses and pettiness of the many
absolute sovereignties of modern Europe, and to blame
Luther and the Reformation for our present woes.
This, I think, is definitely unfair. The great schism
undoubtedly hastened the dissolution of the medieval
European civilization, but the splendid dream of the
great Popes partially realized in the Middle Ages was
already in the throes of disintegration. It was the
pre-existence of nationalism that made Luther's work
possible ; for it rallied to his standard on patriotic
grounds many of the German princes who had no very
deep understanding of his religious faith. Yet, since
Sweden and the Netherlands may be said to owe their
national existence to the great schism, we can clearly
trace the influence of Luther even in the international
situation of to-day.

I must conclude. Luther was a prophetic figure

F

and a religious reformer.   Protestantism springs largely
from his work.   With Protestantism as a moral and
religious influence upon the modern spirit I have not
been directly concerned.   The modern spirit itself is
neither Protestant nor Catholic, but secularist.   But I
have very briefly indicated how democracy, capitalism
and nationalism, typical manifestations of the modern
spirit, have been influenced by the work of Luther.
Protestantism may not take credit for all the merits
and triumphs of the modern spirit, so neither may
Protestantism be blamed where its forms have been
adopted without their deep religious content.

Luther was rather a Catholic reformer than a sponsor
of the modern spirit.   In his political outlook, his
distrust of individualism and private inspirations, in
his thunderings against rational theology and against
the great principle of St. Thomas that the natural
reason is the handmaid of faith,[1] he seems the incarnate
denial of modern ways of thought.   He was a man of
many faults and grievous blindnesses, but a truly great
man.   There are, as we have seen, nations which may
be said to owe their existence to him ; the political and
economic life of the whole world since has been profoundly affected by what he did ; in the field of religion
he seems to be one of the great prophetic figures of
Christian story, and, if he be called heretic because he
saw one truth to the virtual exclusion of all others,
even his enemies are free to admit that the truth he
saw was a great and saving truth.   ' I will call this
Luther a true Great Man,' says Carlyle, ' great in
intellect, in courage, affection and integrity ; one of
our most lovable and precious men.   Great, not as a
hewn obelisk, but as an Alpine mountain—so simple,
honest, spontaneous, not setting up to be great at all ;
there for quite another reason than being great !

---

[1] *Naturalis ratio subservit fidei.*   v. Heiler, op. cit., p. 166.

Ah yes, unsubduable granite, piercing far and wide into the heavens ; yet in the clefts of it fountains, green beautiful valleys with flowers ! A right Spiritual Hero and Prophet ; once more, a true Son of Nature and Fact, for whom these centuries, and many that are to come yet, will be thankful to Heaven.'

If the great schism was a disaster, the blame for it cannot be laid chiefly at Luther's door ; if the religious principle for which he stood has been secularized in the course of time, that does not invalidate his prophetic message. He came at a time when the great and splendid medieval civilization, the offspring of the medieval Church, was breaking up. We live in an age when that civilization is breaking up which has largely been the creation of Protestantism. I cannot doubt that to the Christian Church and to none other power it will be given to build up a new and better civilization for the age that is being born. God grant us a prophet who may lead us into that new task !

## V

## NEWTON

## (1642—1727)

## By H. Levy, M.A., D.Sc., F.R.S.E.

*Professor of Mathematics, Imperial College of Science and Technology*

A GLANCE at a chronological table would show us that Newton was born in 1642 and died in 1727. It would show us more than that. It would show us that the year he was born the Civil War broke out in England ; not simply a fight between two rival gangs, but a clash between a rising culture that had its strength in the towns and among the growing merchant class, and a waning culture representing the relics of a vanishing feudalism—a waning culture that believed in the Divine Right of Kings. We should see, too, that Descartes and Leibniz, Spinoza, Voltaire, Rousseau and William Harvey also lived during Newton's lifetime. These are all significant facts for us. For they suggest to us that Newton, according to the judgement of history, came into being much earlier than Christmas Day, 1642, and that 1727, the year of his death, was not the end of Newton.

Now if a man is great, particularly if he is a great scientist, he must belong to his own times. He must belong to his own age in two ways : his work has to draw nourishment and inspiration from the intellectual and social needs of his day ; and it also has to point the way to further developments. The great man is he who, rising above the swirl and welter of his own day, can separate those things which are passing and parochial from those which are permanent and universal. The great man must be able to rise above what Professor Whitehead has called ' his patch of immediacy.' When we do find such a man it is extraordinarily interesting for us to examine his life and outlook, his work and his career. Newton was one of these great men.

First let me give you a few facts about him. His people were small farmers in Lincolnshire, but his father died shortly before he was born. At the age of nine he was sent to Grantham School, and he lodged there with an apothecary, receiving board in return for work done. He seems always to have led a rather lone life, unable to enter into social intercourse, or to engage in social discussion. He was a celibate, mentally and physically, throughout his life insensible to passion. At the age of nineteen he went to Cambridge as a poor student, receiving tuition in return for doing menial tasks. The life at Cambridge suited his temperament. He could read on his own without being compelled to attend lectures. When he was twenty-three he left Cambridge, at the time when the university was closed during the Great Plague, and for two years, 1665–1666, he lived at his birthplace, Woolsthorpe.

Newton's discoveries may be grouped under three heads —his investigations in optics and light, his dynamical and gravitational discoveries, and his invention of the differential and integral calculus. Newton himself tells us that these three fields of thought were well mapped out and thoroughly understood by him in those two years away from Cambridge. This means that between the ages of twenty-three and twenty-five Newton made the three principal discoveries on which his fame, the fame of one of the greatest scientists of all time, was to rest. The remainder of his scientific life was spent in working out the implications of these three groups of discoveries. He went back to Cambridge and stayed there till 1696, when at the age of fifty-four he was appointed warden of the Mint. On his appointment his scientific work, to all intents and purposes, ceased abruptly. (This is a significant fact, and I want to say more about it when we have considered in greater detail the work Newton carried through, and what his work meant for the age in which he lived.)

Let us consider for a few minutes the social environment into which Newton was born. (Almost a century before he was born that social environment which was to have need of a Newton began to find its setting.) The darkness of the Middle Ages had almost passed. The towns with their rising merchant and manufacturing classes were rapidly gaining in wealth and economic strength, and the spirit of liberty of thought and freedom of expression was beginning to show itself. Moreover a new outlook towards the world outside this island was being stimulated by the growth of transport and navigation ; there was an increased security for sea-craft, and merchandise was being sent to distant places. The working of metals and the beginnings of various industries made for a similar change of outlook. An age of discovery had begun, and with it came criticism of old-fashioned doctrines which no longer fitted the needs of the times. The successful outcome of the Civil War in England set the seal on this new mood.

What has all this to do with Newton ? You may say that after all he was not interested in the mundane matters of commerce, in methods of metal working, in manufacturing processes, in wars and politics. You may say that in spirit he was only concerned with probing the depths of solar space with highly abstract problems of the calculus, with the theory of gravitation and the behaviour of light. You may think of him as the pure scientist, interested only in abstractions. But let us see.

In 1669, four years after his return to Cambridge, we find him writing in a letter to a young student friend, Francis Aston, who was about to go on a tour of Europe, that he must diligently study the mechanics of steering and navigating ships, that he must survey all the fortresses, their construction, powers of resistance, advantages in defence, and that he must generally acquaint himself with war organization. Newton urges him to examine specially the natural resources of each country, particularly metals and minerals, and to study the methods used in refining these metals from their ores. Was it a fact, he asks him, that in Bohemia there were rivers containing gold, and did they derive the gold by amalgamating it with mercury? He must visit the factory in Holland for polishing glasses. He must discover how the Dutch protected their vessels from rot during their voyages to India, and he must discover whether pendulum clocks were of much use in determining longitude during ocean voyages. In particular he must always look out for any method of transforming one metal into another; and Newton explains what might be the processes that were being used in such transmutations. He asks Francis Aston to consider this question, particularly in relation to copper, which was so much in demand at that time both in the casting of cannon and as a medium of exchange in trade.

You must realize, of course, that science as we know it to-day was then in its infancy. There were no lines of demarcation between one field and another, and Newton the mathematician was also Newton the physicist, the chemist, the metallurgist. Newton's preoccupation with the transmutation of base metals into gold—a preoccupation which lasted him all his lifetime, and stood him in good stead when he entered the Mint—is a very good illustration of the remains of the old alchemist spirit.

You often hear nowadays about the pursuit of science as a pure study for its own sake. I am not quite sure the phrase has any meaning, but whatever meaning there may be in it is a comparatively new feature, and arises from the extreme specialization which has overtaken science. Newton had a realistic outlook. He saw clearly that the problems of science were not engineered in men's minds—they arose from the difficulties of practice. He saw that if his science was to be successful it must emerge from these difficulties, and be related to them. He had no parochial ideas about the purity of the study. His greatness largely consisted in being able to take the confusion of facts and fancies which constituted practice and to strip the relevant from the irrelevant. His letter to Francis Aston is an indication of the questions whose solutions he considered important. The catalogue is significant of the spirit of his time. It would not be uninteresting to compare the corresponding advice which would be given by a professor of mathematics to-day to one of his students about to undertake such a tour.

Newton was not alone in making this close association between his scientific pursuits and the needs of his day. Remember that Galileo, who died the year Newton was born, assisted the merchant princes by the provision of telescopes for navigation purposes, that Spinoza was developing his philosophy as he ground their lenses, that Descartes, attempting to produce a compromise between science and theology, was evolving a mathematical method that found its origin in his practice as a gunnery officer.

The period into which Newton was born saw the struggle for the possession of the scientist between a rising merchant and industrial class changing the social order on the one hand, and the institutions of established belief still wedded to the spirit of feudalism on the other, but I think Newton's letter to Francis Aston shows that the new knowledge of the material world was stirring the scientists. Newton was not, in any modern sense, an engineer, although as a youth he was much given to the construction of mechanical toys. But mechanization was in the air. Mechanical science was coming of age. The principle of the pump had been rediscovered and was being applied in a variety of ways. Barometers and clockwork mechanisms were making their appearance. Galileo's primitive thermoscopes were being developed into accurate thermometers. Men were acquiring the measuring habit, the power of exact observation. Perhaps some of you may be surprised to hear that in 1666 a patent was taken out for a steam engine. In 1657 the Dutch investigator, Huygens, had patented his clock, and a little later Hooke added his device of the escapement, and a new means was forthcoming for the accurate measurement of the movements of the stars. As far back as 1629 William Harvey had written his tract on the circulation of the blood, a wholly mechanical description of a life process.

You will see that the time was ripe for a completely mechanical statement about the movement of the heavenly bodies—a description stripped of all reference to mysticism. Of course, I am not going to suggest that those who sought mechanical explanations of things that had been previously shrouded in mystery were themselves free of mysticism. Newton himself had the conventional outlook of his time and his attitude was the common one. Nevertheless these scientists propounding mechanical explanations were by their actions unconsciously changing the conventional dogmatic outlook in readiness for the generation which was to succeed them.

If you consider again the subjects which Newton recommended for study to his friend you will get an idea of the problems that would naturally engage the attention of a mathematical physicist of Newton's time. Such problems as these would naturally emerge—optical questions arising from the use of telescopes, the problem of tides for navigational purposes, the motion of projectiles and of large bodies under the influence of forces of propulsion and resistance. The scientific man would naturally be led to consider predictions about the positions of the planets. Well, as you know, these were the very problems with which Newton's name will be always associated.

I don't want to suggest that Newton deliberately chose these topics simply because they had application in practical life. I am merely suggesting that Newton belonged essentially to his age, and that these were in fact the problems of his age. Moreover, I ask you to remember that when he was offered a post in the Mint, knowing that his mathematical work would definitely come to an end, he accepted it without so much as an expressed regret, and as you know the moment he stepped into the Mint his creative scientific work ceased.

A sidelight on his character is given in a letter which he wrote at the age of thirty-three to Collins. In this letter he says that he had begun ' to find mathematical speculations at least dry, if not barren '—this from one of the greatest mathematicians of all time. One gains the impression from a study of his life that he was a man with stupendous but cold talent, a man with a magnificently powerful intellect, relentlessly chawing up the scientific puzzles of his day without any evidence that they roused in him that consuming fire which makes the scientist brother to the artist.

Newton's abiding interest was a strange relic of medievalism—how to transmute the baser metals into gold. Moreover he was not a person who strove for honour or rushed to publish his discoveries to a waiting world. It was the least important of his discoveries that he announced first—his work in optics. The theory of gravitation which we always associate with Newton's name had to be coaxed from him—I had almost said torn from him—by Halley, the astronomer. And his discovery of the calculus was not

announced until many years after Leibniz had indepen-
dently discovered, and perfected, the same process. He
kept it as a sort of trade secret by means of which to
investigate his discoveries. A queer fellow, Newton.

So much for the effect of his environment on Newton.
Let us now turn to a study of the actual contributions
which Newton made to science, in order that we may find
out what was the effect of Newton on society. Let us
briefly scrutinize his optical discoveries first. In optics—
the study of light—Newton opened up a region of study
which was entirely new. Before his time light was something peculiar, in a sense mystical. The telescope makers
and lens grinders knew something of the properties of
light, but it was never separated even for them from a
certain spiritual quality. Roemer had not yet made the
discovery that light travels at a definite speed. Light
seemed to appear everywhere instantaneously, and the
spiritual significance of its character was judged from the
heavenly sign of the rainbow. However, certain aspects
of light were seen to be measurable—a ray of light was
clearly bent in passing through a lens, and the amount of
bending could be measured. But no one imagined that
the colour of light could be measured. Colour seemed to
be purely an aesthetic matter. I dare say you know that
the scholastics—I refer to those who only *thought* about
science and didn't *do* any—the scholastics had already
decreed that things had two kinds of qualities, primary
and secondary. The primary qualities, things like size,
shape and solidity, were *in* the object ; the secondary
characteristics, qualities like warmth, colour, beauty, did
not exist in the object, but in the eyes of those beholding
them, i.e., in the subject. This view served a useful purpose ; it prevented a premature search for specific
qualities before the instruments for investigating them
were to hand. You must have a thermometer, for
example, before you can estimate the ' warmth ' of a

body. But this division into secondary and primary qualities was unfortunate in that it separated off in advance a region which scientists were discouraged from studying. Colour was one of those forbidden regions. When Newton began working with telescopes he soon found it necessary to examine this problem of colour in order to remove certain blurring effects. So he set to work with a glass prism and, as every one knows, he discovered that when a beam of colourless sunlight was passed through it the beam was split up into a spectrum of coloured light. He also found that by passing this rainbow back through the prism he could reproduce colourless sunlight again. It was soon apparent to him that each beam of coloured light of which white light was composed was bent by a characteristic amount in passing through the glass prism. Here, then, was a quality of coloured light which could be measured.

This seems a simple enough discovery, but I think most scientists will agree that it is one of the most fundamental in the whole history of optical science. From it has arisen the whole technique of spectrum analysis, which as you probably know, has brought the sun and stars into our laboratories, and given us knowledge about their internal constitution, and about their temperatures. It has also led to the discovery of new elements, first detected in the sun's atmosphere by means of the spectroscope.

Newton's greatest work, however, did not lie in the field of optics. His main contribution was in mechanics. The great debt which we owe him is the impetus which he gave to mechanical ideas. His work in mechanics is to be found in his great work the *Principia*. The problems there have a geometrical setting, proposition succeeding proposition in logical order. But the book did not represent a sudden break with the past. It owed much to the work of his predecessors. After all, gravitation and the laws of motion were topical. Galileo had

already established the fact that all bodies fall to the
earth with the same steadily increasing speed, irrespective of their weight. By experimenting with balls rolling
down slightly inclined planes Galileo had also been led to
the conclusion that a body once set in motion on a level
will continue, if friction is absent, to move forward with
the same speed.

Now this in effect is Newton's first law of motion.
Galileo had in fact destroyed the belief that a cannon-ball
was urged forward by an internal mysterious urge. He
showed from his observations that the motion of the
cannon-ball could be described in precise mathematical
terms. The ice thus broken for him, Newton showed
that it was possible to treat all mechanical movements
from a mathematical point of view. The task for him
was to devise the appropriate mathematics. Kepler
had also paved the way. Kepler knew that the planets
moved approximately in circles round the sun, and that
you could calculate these movements by simple rules.
*Why* the planets kept to their paths no one knew, although it was generally believed to be an illustration of
the perfect working of the laws of God : a mysterious
inner drive kept the planets to their courses.

The curious medley of scientific analysis and mystical
explanation which found expression in the days before
Newton makes strange reading for us. But the time was
ripe for a new synthesis stripped of mysticism. It is to
Newton we owe this synthesis. We recognize that the
work of Galileo on falling bodies, of Copernicus on the
circling of planets round the sun, and Kepler's arith-
metical rules for planetary motions were all manifestations of the general principle of gravitational attraction.
In stating his famous law of inverse squares Newton
calculated that the earth would rotate in an ellipse round
the sun with the sun as focus, and he made numerous
predictions about other solar bodies, all from the same

general principle. Moreover, he went on to show that if the inverse square law is true for every pair of particles in the universe, a spherical body would act as if its whole mass were situated at a *point* at its centre. And so he paved the way for dealing with much more complex situations. By extending mechanical ideas into interplanetary space he introduced order and system where chaos and mystery had reigned before.

As soon as he had made this first synthesis the solution to innumerable other puzzles began to appear. He saw, for example, that the earth must be flattened at its poles, and that, therefore, the force of gravity at the poles must be less than that at the equator. And then he solved the puzzle of tidal flow, calculating how much would be due to the moon's attraction, and how much to the sun's attraction. Further, he was able to show how, from observing the shape of a planet, it was possible to estimate the time occupied by day and night on that planet.

It is almost incredible that any one man could have achieved so much, and it is more incredible still when you remember that all this was accomplished in a small fraction of his lifetime. You have got to remember that not only did he bring together and reduce to order an enormous mass of very diverse observations, but that he subjected them to analysis by a totally new mathematical technique which he invented—the differential and integral calculus.

I cannot tell you now what the differential calculus is with any hope of your understanding it. Briefly it is a method of finding the speed and acceleration of a moving body from a knowledge of its position at successive instants of time. Anyway, it was a method that had to be invented before Newton's second law of motion could be applied, and it was necessary that this piece of mathematical machinery should be invented before the laws of mechanics could be fully exploited. I must ask you to forgive me for not going into any greater detail, but after all I am a professor of mathematics, and you must allow me to suppose that I am unintelligible on my own subject.

But I shall carry you with me when I say that throughout the whole 250 years since his death, Newton's laws of motion, together with the use of the calculus, have provided the basis on which all scientific advance has rested. Without it even the more recent developments, associated with relativity and the quantum theory, would have been impossible—in spite of the fact that in certain respects they replace Newton's laws.

I want to rub in this point again. The calculus was bound to come because the need for it was being increasingly felt, and because mathematics was sufficiently advanced to supply the need. It is more than certain that a great deal of the *Principia* would in any case have been discovered within a few years. Readers of this book may find it worth while to compare my point of view, that history produces crises that show up great men, with the point of view of other contributors in this series who put the great men first and say that they produced their age.

Some justification for my belief may be found in a study of Newton's contemporaries. I have already shown you that Newton owed a great deal to his immediate predecessors. His own teacher, Barrow, had already broken up the ground considerably, and Leibniz's regrettable squabble with Newton, and later the trouble with Hooke over priority for his theories, show clearly that the solution of such problems was urgent. I do not want to enter into discussion here about those unfortunate squabbles. My point is made when I remind you that they existed. Newton doesn't shine in them. He would not brook criticism, and apparently he did not possess that human and sympathetic mind which enabled Kepler to applaud the discoveries of Galileo and Darwin to place himself equal with Wallace.   The squabbles, however, do not detract from Newton's greatness as a mathematician, and the great marvel still remains that he as an individual contributed so much.   He was, and always will remain, a colossal figure in the history of mathematics.

Having said that, I am going to state that Newton himself possessed no philosophy worthy of the name. In the practice of his scientific work he was definitely a mechanist, and a successful one—measurable effects expressed in terms of measurable causes.   Nothing was excluded from the possibility of his mechanistic approach.   He had the supreme gift of using mathematics in every conceivable situation.   But on the other hand his statements about science were experimental in outlook.   He always said that he wouldn't touch hypotheses that could never be tested, but his laws of motions are riddled with them.   He introduces ideas like absolute position and absolute speed and an evenly flowing time, none of which could be tested.   Newton didn't trouble over-much about the philosophical difficulties and therein lay his strength, for science was struggling to throw off a dead weight of useless philosophy, and needed, above everything else, confidence inspired by results on a useful, rather than a philosophical, basis.   Science had to prove its worth.

In the struggle between the new science and the old religion Newton personally found an easy compromise. To Newton the system of mechanical laws, the process of mechanical cause and effect, to which he had given such a great impetus, definitely required a Great Mechanic who ran the system.   God was outside the universe, but certain duties were assigned to Him. For example, one of God's duties was to prevent the fixed stars from falling together. This problem was an unsolved one in Newton's scientific scheme, and so in his naïve way Newton safeguarded his theology from the destructive attack of mechanistic philosophy, by inserting his God as one of the forces in his machine.

Before I stop I must direct your notice to the statement which one often hears that Newton's work has been overthrown by Einstein. Einstein, of course, would be the last person to assert this, for it is true only in the very restricted sense. In science every time a new and more embracing law is discovered, it is because the unseen limitations of previous work have been at last exposed to view. Einstein did not overthrow Newton but stood on his shoulders, just as Newton stood on the shoulders of giants before him. Einstein's work has thrown into relief the limitations under which Newton worked. Einstein is the necessary continuation of Newton, but Newton's countless astronomical predictions still stand, and the mechanical principles in engineering, chemistry and experimental physics, developed from his work, are still applicable within their respective fields. Newton's method of attack—the separation of a problem into a mathematically measurable cause and a mathematically predictable effect—is likely to remain the method of science for countless generations to come.

## VI

# FROM AQUINAS TO NEWTON

## By John Macmurray

BY this time we have got well under way in our study of the development of the Modern Spirit. We have studied Aquinas and Luther and Newton. That brings us to the most convenient break in the whole period which we are studying. We are on the eve of the development of democracy and the social changes which are connected with it. So it is an opportune point at which to pause and take stock of our position. We are trying to see these three great men in relation to one another, and in relation to the world as it is to-day. We begin to *feel* the difference between them, and between the stages of history which they represent. But it is difficult to get the differences clear enough to see the direction in which the modern spirit is moving from Aquinas to Newton. I should like to help, if I can, in this difficulty and to do it, so far as possible, by direct reference to what is contained in the three preceding chapters.

Let us start by comparing our impressions of St. Thomas and of Newton. They have one thing in common which makes it easy to compare them. They are both concerned with the increase of knowledge. Their claim to be great men rests primarily upon their efforts to discover truth. They are men of knowledge.

Now I should like to ask a question. Which of these two men comes nearer to our own conception of a man of knowledge? I am inclined to think that after reading these two chapters you will all be inclined to say : 'Thomas Aquinas,' though perhaps this is not the answer that you would have expected to have to give. Let me remind you of one or two points that emerged. Aquinas turned his back on a life of wealth and power in order to become a poor scholar. He spent his life in the pursuit of truth and nothing else. When he was called in to help in great practical decisions he did so. But he showed no desire for honour or power in that connexion, and he wanted always to get back to his studies. Newton, on the other hand, found mathematics in the long run rather a bore, and when he became an official of the Mint, that was the end of his scientific discoveries. That does not sound at all like the typical scholar or man of knowledge who had devoted his life to truth. Again, both Father D'Arcy and Professor Levy have quoted letters of advice from the great man to a young student and friend, which form a remarkable contrast. Aquinas counsels diligence, purity of conscience, reticence. 'Don't gad about,' he says. 'Fix in your mind everything good that is said, make an effort thoroughly to understand whatever you read and hear. In all doubt seek to penetrate to the truth !' That is what you would expect from a man who has given himself up to knowledge, and for whom the search for truth is the highest of all duties. Now think of Newton's advice. His young friend must diligently study the mechanics of navigation, the theory and practice of warfare, the natural resources of countries, particularly in respect of metals and minerals, and the methods of dealing with the ore. He is to be particularly on the look-out for methods of transforming one metal into another.

That reminds us of Newton's perpetual interest in gold. Could there be a greater contrast between these two conceptions of a student's business? So I put my question again : 'Does Aquinas or Newton come nearest to what we think a man who is devoted to the pursuit of knowledge ought to be ? ' And this time I really expect the vast majority of readers to say : ' Aquinas.'

But that does not end the matter. It is true that Aquinas fits better into our conception of the real man of knowledge. On the other hand we must not forget that for all that Newton was the man who made the crucial discoveries upon which modern science rests and which has transformed our lives and our forms of social and political organization. It will not do to conclude that Newton was not a great man in the field of knowledge, while Aquinas was. That would just be palpably untrue. Perhaps it means rather that one of the greatest changes which has taken place between Aquinas and Newton is a change in the nature of knowledge and its relation to life. The first conclusion that I feel inclined to draw is a different one. It is that our conception of what a man of knowledge ought to be is still medieval, and that we have discovered one very important point in the modern spirit in which it remains unchanged from medieval times. Our ideal of knowledge is still the ideal which inspired the searchers after truth in the Middle Ages. The actual knowledge which the modern world has produced and in which it is really interested is a different kind of knowledge which rests upon a different motive and which does not correspond to our cultural conception of what knowledge and its devotees ought to be. Let me quote a passage from Professor Levy. ' You often hear, nowadays, about the pursuit of science as a pure study for its own sake. I am not quite sure the phrase has any meaning, but whatever meaning there may be in it is a comparatively new feature, and arises from the extreme specialization which is overtaking science.' Might I suggest that the talk about pure science for its own sake is really the result of interpreting science and picturing the scientist in terms of Aquinas and not of Newton?

The second comment I want to make here is that it is no use to say that Aquinas was right and Newton was wrong, or vice versa. Instead, we must notice that the kind of knowledge that Aquinas was seeking was very different from the kind of knowledge that Newton was after. Different kinds of knowledge require to be sought through different methods, and require different men and different motives for their development. In other words, Aquinas and the world of which he is a symbol were interested in something quite different from Newton and the modern world which he represents. It is this difference in interest and the difference in motives which underlies it which measures the distance that we have travelled from Aquinas to Newton. The things that Newton thinks it important to discover are not the things that Aquinas thought it important to discover. That is the real difference.

Obviously a very fundamental change has come over the European spirit to produce the conception of what it is important to know that speaks in Newton's letter of advice to a young student. Let us ask what this change is. I think that if we now turn our attention to the talk on Luther we may get some light, because a great change came over the spirit of Luther in the course of his life. Dr. Micklem mentioned that Luther attacked St. Thomas Aquinas for his belief in reason. Luther did that after his conversion. He would not, I think, have done it during the earlier part of his career. Luther started with a passionate devotion to the world of which Aquinas is the clearest expression. Later in life he repudiated his allegiance to that world, and had a great deal to do with its destruction. Like Aquinas, Luther chose the life of a poor monk. In his cell he went to extreme lengths in his effort to subdue the natural headstrong energy of his mind and body to the conception of life and the rule of faith of which Aquinas was the great expositor. More than once, if we can believe the reports, he brought himself to the point of death by his fastings and penances in order to achieve that sainthood that rested so easily upon the calm spirit of St. Thomas. He tried hard to become the kind of man that would fit in to the ideal that St. Thomas so skilfully set out. What lay behind this desperate effort of self-denial and self-repression ? It was fear ; fear of sin, fear of hell, fear of the Devil and the power of the Devil. Now think of what Dr. Micklem had to say about Luther after he had repudiated this effort. He describes him as a man of splendid and indomitable courage, both physical and moral. ' There is about him,' he says, ' an abandon, a gaiety, almost a boyish irresponsibility. He was utterly carefree, illimitably generous ; he lived from day to day and recked little of consequences.' He quotes von Schubert as saying : ' There is a marvellous overflowing freedom from care in this Luther.' As for his fear of the Devil ; we have the story of how he woke up in the night conscious that Satan himself was in the room, and said : ' Oh, it's only you, is it ? ' and fell asleep again. Something has happened to Luther which has changed the whole spirit of the man, and that change is marked by his repudiation of the world of which Thomas Aquinas is our symbol. In escaping from that world Luther escaped from fear, and became one of the men who impresses us, if by nothing else, by his indomitable fearlessness.

Luther had escaped from fear. But how? He would have put it himself by saying that he had discovered that we are saved by faith, not by works. How could that make such a change in a man, and turn fear and self-repression into a joyous, carefree abandon? Simply because it put an end to his preoccupation with himself, and his desperate efforts to change himself into the medieval ideal of what a saint should be. That preoccupation with his own salvation had turned all his energy and vitality inwards. It had made him self-centred. But when he realized, as he would have put it, that his salvation and the salvation of the world was the free gift of God's grace, and not something that he had to earn, a great light shone in on the darkness. He didn't have to worry about himself any more, he had only to accept his redemption as a gift and be grateful. Then he found himself in a world which was not hostile but friendly, or, as Dr. Micklem quoted: ' then as now, in the hands of Almighty God.' What was there to be afraid of? As a result he found himself no longer interested in himself, no longer the centre of his own world, and the energy and vitality in him was free to flow out in glad, spontaneous activity. And that enormous energy which was set free set the world moving. It has been moving ever since.

That change in Luther's life is itself a symbol of the change from the medieval to the modern world. It was a change from man's interest in man to man's interest in the world. It was a release from fear and bondage, from the effort to keep things as they were, to maintain something, into an effort to act upon the world, to discover something and to create something new. What happened to Luther happened in another way—a less important way—to Galileo. For Galileo, as for the world of his time in the Middle Ages, our earth was the centre of the material universe. One day he found that Copernicus doubted this. Perhaps it wasn't true. Perhaps it was the sun that stood still while the earth circled round it. Galileo became convinced of this, and proceeded to publish this new belief. An old tradition, which symbolized the position well, even if, as scholars tell us, there is no good ground for believing that it is historically true, tells us that the medieval world tried to silence Galileo as it tried to silence Luther ; that he was prosecuted ; that he formally recanted, but was not convinced ; that he left the scene of his recantation muttering to himself : ' *Eppur si muove* ! '—' But it does move all the same.' The modern world has agreed. Copernicus and Galileo had thrown the centre of the world outside itself, and so set the world moving. And it has been moving ever since.

Now, perhaps, we can come back to our contrast between St. Thomas and Newton, and understand it better. For all his immense scholarship and learning, for all his devotion to knowledge, St. Thomas lives in a world where man is shut up in himself. As a man of knowledge he is interested in truth. Newton, on the other hand, is not interested in truth, he is interested in the world outside himself. That is the heart of the difference between the two men, as it is the heart of the difference between the medieval and the modern world. The secret of science is that it secures knowledge not by being interested in knowledge, but by being interested in the things that knowledge is about. To be interested in truth is really to be interested in your own thinking and worried about getting it right. At the bottom of it lies the fear of being wrong, and the fear of the dreadful consequences that may result from being wrong. It means that you are interested in yourself and not in the world, even when you seem to be interested in the world outside you. It has often been said that the way to get pleasure is to forget about it and be interested in something that isn't pleasure. In the same way we might say that the way to get knowledge is to forget about it and be interested in something that is not knowledge. It is this that we find in Newton. He has something of that same buoyant carelessness that we find in the later Luther, the modern Luther. He has got away from the interest in himself and his knowledge and his investigations to an interest in the new things that were happening in the world around him. And the result is that he gained, one might almost say accidentally, a knowledge which flows out into action, and which has revolutionized the world.

It may seem that I was exaggerating when I suggested that the basis of the kind of knowledge of which St. Thomas was one of the most illustrious exponents was fear. Let me quote again from Father D'Arcy's talk. 'Just as now,' he said, 'there were then conservatives of the die-in-the-ditch type who were affronted by the whirlwind energy of youth and the swift development of thought on social and intellectual matters. There existed, too, dialecticians and sophists and revolutionaries who gave legitimate cause for anxiety. . . . Intemperance and social anarchy were real dangers.' Notice that phrase 'gave legitimate cause for anxiety.' The fear of social change shines through it. Aquinas laboured in the service of that anxiety. Luther discovered that the effort to preserve that anxious world was not worth the candle. I think I can hear him say, revolutionary that he was : 'Legitimate cause for anxiety! There is no legitimate cause for anxiety. Now, as always, we are in the hands of Almighty God.'

## VII

ROUSSEAU

(1712—1778)

By LEONARD WOOLF

MY task in this chapter is both easy and difficult. It is easy because every one agrees that no man had a greater effect upon the modern spirit than Rousseau. The difficulty is that he had so much to do with making us all what we are to-day that I hardly know how to squeeze his life and works into a few pages. I must therefore plunge straight into my subject.

Rousseau was born two hundred and twenty years ago, in 1712. He lived sixty-six years, dying in 1778 or roughly one hundred and fifty years ago. He died, you will observe, eleven years before the French Revolution, an important fact to remember, because that revolution marks one of the great dividing lines between the old and the modern spirit. Before 1789 the old world, the world of the Middle Ages and feudalism, and kings and aristocrats and authority, political and religious, was fighting for its life, but it was still on top and all-powerful ; in the French Revolution it received a blow from which it never really recovered. In 1789 the modern world was born ; the modern spirit became self-conscious ; the modern

man, the ordinary man in the street whom we know
to-day, came into existence.

It is important to get these few dates into your
mind before we look at Rousseau's life. For Rousseau,
you will observe, never lived in the modern world, the
world of the modern spirit—he was born and he died
in the ancient world. And the reason why he did
so much to destroy the ancient world and bring the
modern spirit to birth was just this : that besides being
a great genius, he was essentially a modern man, a
man of the nineteenth century, born a hundred years
before his time. He thought and felt and wanted to
live, not as his contemporaries thought and felt and
lived, but in the way that hundreds of thousands of
ordinary men and women think and feel and would
like to live to-day. Let me give you one small, perhaps
unimportant, instance straight away, though I shall
give you others which are more imposing later on.
To my mind, hiking is very characteristic of the
modern spirit. Professor Macmurray in the introductory chapter told us that one of the two governing
ideas at the root of the development of the modern
world is the idea of the freedom of the individual.
Now these fundamental ideas, which are said to be
at the root of the spirit of an age, may be seen, if we
use our eyes, working in small things as well as in
great, and it is just as interesting and illuminating to
observe the spirit of an age influencing people in the
way in which they spend their half-holidays as in the
way in which they govern an empire. If you consider
the hiker and his passion for hiking, you will see, I
think, that his state of mind is not unconnected with
this modern passion for the freedom of the individual.
There are, indeed, people whose passion for freedom is
so strong, who find the restraints upon their individuality in the respectable life of our towns so irksome,

that they voluntarily take to the road and become tramps and beggars by vocation, and respectable people call them vagrants and vagabonds. And the real hiker is always temporarily an amateur tramp, vagrant and vagabond. The important thing to notice is that Rousseau was the first hiker. His great autobiography, *The Confessions,* is full of references to his delight in tramping, to the sense of freedom and of being oneself which one gets from hiking, but there is one passage in particular which will show you how modern Rousseau is in spirit, and how impossible it was for him to find any one among his contemporaries to sympathize with him.

At the age of sixteen he ran away from his home in Geneva, and fell into the hands of some Roman Catholic proselytizers who sent him from Savoy over the Alps to Italy, in order that he might be converted there to the true faith. He made the journey on foot, and he tells us that he never forgot the delights of that journey, which left him with a passion for everything connected with it, particularly mountains and hiking. ' It was only in my happy days,' he says, ' that I travelled on foot ; it always delighted me. Later, duties, business, luggage, forced me to play the gentleman and to take a carriage ; troubles, worries and boredom entered the carriage with me, and, while before in my travels I had only felt the pleasure of travelling, I now only felt the desire to get to my destination.' There you have Rousseau, and there you also have the modern hiker. But in 1728, and even later still, in 1750, no one except Rousseau was a hiker with the modern spirit. He tells us that afterwards in Paris, when he was no longer a vagabond, but already a famous man and the friend of famous men like the great Diderot and Grimm, he tried to find two companions with the same tastes as himself who would join

him in a walking tour or hike through France and Italy
which should last for a year. He could find no one to
join him, and the reason was, though he himself was
not aware of it, that the modern spirit at that time
existed only in Rousseau himself.

This love of travelling on foot is so characteristic of
Rousseau, it springs from such fundamental things in
his mind, that it would be possible, without exaggeration, to show you its connexion with almost the whole
of his teaching and the whole of his influence upon the
generations which came after him. Note, for instance,
in the passage which I quoted from *The Confessions*,
the remark that later on in his life he had to travel in
carriages and ' play the gentleman.' Rousseau loved
travelling on foot because it kept him a man of the
people, among the common people. You will remember that Professor Macmurray told you that the second
governing idea which lay at the root of the development
of the modern world is equality, and I think he was
right if by equality we mean the social equality of all
individuals. You can see this modern idea of equality
in Rousseau's attitude towards the common people
and his misery at having to ' play the gentleman.' He
lived in a world in which the whole of society was based
on a system of social inequality, in which your rights and
your value and your privileges and your duties depended upon your birth, upon the class into which
you happened to be born. States were organized and
governed not in the interests of ordinary people, but
in the interests of kings, aristocrats, gentlemen and
privileged classes. No one had a greater influence in
breaking down this system and in infecting the world
with the modern spirit of social equality than Rousseau.
' It is the common people,' he wrote in *Emile*, his
great work on education, for the writing of which
the French Government hounded him out of France,

'it is the common people who make up the human race ; what is not the common people is hardly worth considering.' To-day nearly every one, even the most conservative and reactionary, would agree or profess to agree with that remark, but in 1762 it was revolutionary, a trumpet call to the French Revolution.

These two ideas of freedom and equality, both of which are connected with Rousseau's love of hiking, influenced the whole of his life and permeate the whole of his works. His views are so often misrepresented that it is necessary to state quite clearly what he really thought and said. Nearly every one in his day believed, and many people still to-day unconsciously believe, that ordinary men and women are fundamentally bad or stupid, and will therefore always go wrong if left to follow their own inclinations. This belief lies at the root of medieval society, of the religion of nearly all the Churches, and of all governments based on 'authority' and privileged or ruling classes. It is really accepted by all those who hold that discipline should be one of the chief instruments of education, that politically the government should make laws and the people obey them, and that the authority of a Church and the pronouncements of its priests should determine for the common people not only the constitution of the universe, but also what is right and what wrong, and how each of us ought to live. Rousseau taught exactly the opposite doctrine. He held that human beings if left to themselves to follow their own instincts and develop their natural capacities, are good. Therefore, the freer an individual is to follow the dictates of his own personality, 'to live,' as we now say, 'his own life,' the better he is likely to be as an individual ; and the less dictation and authority there is in society, the better will our society be. And closely linked with this doctrine of freedom is his doctrine of equality. He never said, of course, that all men are equal in every way. What he said was that, as individuals, they are all socially of equal value, and should therefore, for purposes of human government, be treated as equal and of equal value. The king, the privileged aristocrat, the priest, has no monopoly of truth or virtue ; truth and virtue are to be found in the heart of the ordinary man if only kings, governments, and priests would give him the opportunity of developing his own capacities. And so it is the common people, not the kings, governing classes, popes, and bishops, who are ' worth considering.'

These views of Rousseau, in the political sphere, lead straight to the modern conception of democracy, and his famous book, *The Social Contract*, in which he applied them to politics, had an enormous influence upon the French Revolution and upon democratic thought in the nineteenth century. There is a little bit of Rousseau's mind still alive to-day in the political ideas of nearly all of us. But he applied these ideas not only to politics but to life generally, and here again he has had immense influence upon us. He tells us that throughout his own life his determination had been ' always to be myself,' and, as I shall show you in a moment, no man ever more bravely put his principles into practice.

This idea of ' living one's own life,' and of the value of ' being one's self,' of developing one's own individuality, is a very modern one. Before Rousseau, hardly any one seems to have had this modern sense of personality and of its value. That was partly because in the ancient world every one regarded himself and other people primarily not as individuals but as members of classes. You were an aristocrat or a common man, a tax collector or a peasant, a Roman Catholic or a heretic, and it was your main duty in life to continue in the estate to which God had called you. The idea that the son of a watchmaker, like Rousseau, had a personality which was of value in itself, that he had a right and duty to live his own life, to be himself, to develop his own capacities no matter where or into what sphere of life they might carry him, to think for himself and determine for himself what was true and what right and wrong, irrespective of authority—such an idea was alien to the ancient world and the kind of society described to you by Father D'Arcy. But this is the idea which lies at the root of Rousseau's life and of all his teaching, whether it is about politics or society or religion or education.

There is one other thing connected with Rousseau's love of hiking which had an immense influence upon the nineteenth century and is still influencing us. He tells us, you will remember, that he never forgot the delights of that first journey on foot over the Alps into Italy, and that it left him with a passion for mountains and scenery. His autobiography proves that what he says was not a pose or an exaggeration, but the literal truth. Rousseau had an intimate and romantic passion for Nature, and that was one reason why he loved hiking. In his autobiography he continually describes his walks or his travels on foot; sometimes it is a picnic with two young girls in the woods, and on the mountain slopes of Savoy, sometimes a long solitary tramp across France from Paris to the Alps. There are few things more beautiful in French prose or poetry than these descriptions of scenery and Nature which are scattered through his writings. But they do not merely prove that Rousseau was a great writer. No one can mistake in them the note of deep and sincere emotion. And that emotion, a feeling that mountains and streams and meadows, and the song of the skylark or the nightingale, are intimately connected with us, that Nature is part of us, and that we are part of Nature, was something new in the world. It played a great part in producing during the latter part of the eighteenth and the beginning of the nineteenth century what we now know as the Romantic Movement in literature.

And now I want to say a few words about Rousseau's actual life, for the way he lived will, I think, make clearer to you the nature of his views, and why he had so much to do with forming the modern spirit. The first thing to notice is that he was a man of the people, the son of a Geneva watchmaker. His family was respectable, but lower middle class, and for many years he lived as the common people were accustomed to live in the first part of the eighteenth century, and often the common people who were not even respectable. It is very important to realize this because it gave to Rousseau understanding of the common people, and an outlook on life which was new in French literature. Before his appearance literature and philosophy and political and religious speculation were provinces of the upper classes, and were often treated as ornaments and objects of patronage for high society. They were therefore very much influenced by the manners and forms of what is called society. Rousseau broke right through that tradition. He paid little attention to good manners whether in life or literature, and he spoke with the voice of the common people about politics, society, religion and education. You will see this nowhere more clearly than in *The Confessions*, probably the greatest autobiography ever written, and certainly the first modern autobiography. In that book in the first paragraph he says that he wishes to show to his fellowmen a man exactly as he naturally is, and that man Rousseau himself. And

H

he is as good as his word, for he wrote what is probably the most truthful book ever written. Rousseau tells us everything about himself, including the dirtiest actions and meanest thoughts that shame and good manners make other men do everything to conceal, even from themselves.

And he had a good many things to confess; there were not a few dirty actions in his life and mean thoughts in his mind. This was partly due to the kind of life which he led until he was thirty, for he was by no means respectable according to the standards of society. His father apprenticed him to an engraver, who treated him with some harshness. He ran away, as I said before, at the age of sixteen from his master, and his home in Geneva, and fell into the hands of Roman Catholic proselytizers who sent him to Italy. There he was converted from Protestantism to Catholicism. During the next twelve years he saw life in many different places and in nearly every grade of society. He was a valet in Italy; he took to the road and became one of those adventurous vagabonds who were rather common in the eighteenth century. At one moment in Switzerland he attached himself to a charlatan who called himself the Archimandrite of Jerusalem, and set out with him for that city, collecting money on the way for the restoration of the Holy Sepulchre. The strange pair did not, however, get very far, for the Archimandrite was soon arrested as an impostor, and the penniless Rousseau had to revert to his original occupation, which was teaching music. He then returned to Savoy, where he lived until he was twenty-eight, with intervals of wandering on foot through France and Switzerland. During those years he worked for a short time in an office, sometimes earned money by being a tutor, and sometimes by teaching music. In 1738 and 1739 he spent most of his time alone in a house which he has made famous, called Les Charmettes, in the depths of the country in a beautiful wooded valley. Those were perhaps the most important years of Rousseau's life, for there, in the rural solitude which he loved, he read innumerable books—on philosophy and religion and science and mathematics and politics—and meditated and formed his views of life and the world and the universe. It was in Les Charmettes, I think, that the watchmaker's son of Geneva educated himself at the age of twenty-six to become the famous Rousseau whom we know as one of the chief makers of the modern spirit.

Three years later he set out to make his fortune in Paris. He still regarded himself as a musician and composer, and that was how he tried to earn a living, not with much success, in Paris. In fact, until he was nearly forty years old he wrote nothing, and lived by doing secretarial work and by copying music. But the point to notice is that all through this period before he became famous, when he was a penniless vagabond, when he was meditating at Les Charmettes, and when he was copying music in Paris, just as later, when he was one of the most famous men in Europe, Rousseau never compromised with his own principles. He determined to live his own life, to ' be myself,' and neither poverty nor obscurity nor the lure of riches or fame ever induced him to give up his independence. He was a passionate man, and extraordinarily sensitive, and he had the awkward habit of saying clearly and often violently whatever was in his mind. In all these things Rousseau belonged to our age, and not to that of Louis XV of France. That was why the great men of his age, like Diderot and D'Alembert and Voltaire, though some of them for a time became his friends, and though they recognized some strange power in himself and his books, were at the same time repulsed, disgusted, and even terrified by him.   They felt instinctively in him the spirit of a new age, and it was alien and horrible to them.   ' The man is mad,' said Diderot and many others.   Towards the end of his life, Rousseau was, it is true, for a time in a condition which was bordering on madness, but essentially he was sane.   But just as he seemed to his contemporaries strange and terrifying, because he belonged not to their age but to ours, so necessarily they and their ways and society exasperated and tortured him.   I doubt whether any of us alive to-day, if we were suddenly transported to the Paris of 1750 with all our modern ideas and feelings, and were condemned to live there and earn our livings—I doubt very much whether many of us would, at the end of ten years, be quite sane.

At the age of thirty-eight Rousseau suddenly wrote a book.   It was not a very good book, but it won him a prize, and it started him off on his career as an author.   It is a remarkable fact that though he lived sixty-six years, he was nearly forty before he wrote anything, and practically all his writing was concentrated in ten years of his life.   He was forty-six before he wrote the *Nouvelle Heloise*, the book which made him famous, and which had an enormous influence upon the development of the novel, and upon European literature generally.   He was fifty when he published his other two great works, the *Contrat Social*, which became the Bible of many of the French Revolutionists and nineteenth-century democrats, and *Emile*, which explained his views on education and religion.

The publication of *Emile* brought Rousseau fame, but it also brought him disaster.   The book is mainly concerned with education.   Rousseau gives in great detail what he considers to be an ideal educational system for a child.   The essential idea underlying it is

that we should rely in education upon freedom and
Nature. To teach children, as is usually done, by
arguments, commands and discipline, produces only
slaves and tyrants ; the right method is to give the
child from his earliest years the utmost possible freedom to learn by experience, and to develop his natural
capacities. Unfortunately, space does not permit me
to deal with Rousseau's views which had an extraordinary effect both upon educational theory and
practice, for I must say one word about his religious
opinions.

In the middle of this book *Emile* he inserted a famous
and beautiful passage about religion. Rousseau was
a believer in God. He was a deist, and he states with
extraordinary sincerity and simplicity the reasons
why he believed in the existence of God. But he
added the reasons why he mistrusted the dogmas and
authority of the Church. To do that in the ancient
world was extremely dangerous. Rousseau's book
was proscribed, and an order made for his arrest. He
fled from France, and for the next six years of his life
he was hounded about Europe in poverty and illness
by the governments and the Church. In 1770 he
returned to Paris, and there for the last eight years of
his life he lived, very poor and lonely, earning a liveli-
hood once more by copying music. Such glimpses as
we have of him in those last years, show him to have
remained what he had always been, a man of immense
independence, in practice true to his principles, determined above all things to live his own life, to ' be
myself.'

If you read books about Rousseau, you will find in
many of them a much more unfavourable account of
Rousseau than I have given you. The reason is that
Rousseau stands for an ideal of individual and social
conduct which horrified the ancient world, and is still

abhorrent to many people. He taught that the individual should aim at developing his own individuality and capacities, keeping close to Nature, living his own life, thinking and acting for himself. And he held that the ideal society would be one in which individuals enjoyed the maximum amount of freedom to live their own lives and to think for themselves, in which they were not regimented by laws and governments, disciplined by their rulers, and told what to believe by their Churches. In the opposition between these views and ideals of Rousseau, and of those who are horrified by him, you will, I suggest, find the main issue raised by this talk, for his views are naturally repugnant to all who consider that authority and discipline are more desirable in government, morals, Churches and education, than freedom, equality and individuality.

# VIII

## GOETHE

### (1749—1832)

### By G. P. GOOCH, M.A., D.Litt., F.B.A.

GOETHE is the transcendent figure in the history of German culture, and the sovereign name in European literature since Shakespeare. His fame has survived all changes of mental habit, and the centenary celebrations last year voiced the abiding gratitude of the world. We paid our homage not only to the dramatist and the poet, the fashioner of imperishable works, but to the thinker, the teacher and the man. The civilization of a people, declares Georg Brandes, may be measured by its appreciation of Goethe. We know him as intimately as Napoleon, and more intimately than any other citizen in the republic of letters. And because we know him so well we can correlate his life and his writings, interpret the phases of his intellectual development in the light of his personal experiences, and watch the growth of his opulent personality. No purely literary approach to the author of *Werther* and *Faust* will suffice, as it has to suffice with Shakespeare. ' I have never shammed,' he remarked to Eckermann. ' I have only written love poems when I have loved.' His writings are fragments of a great confession, revelations of the mind and heart of a master of the art of life.

Happily he is no stranger in England, for no country but his own has studied him so intensively as the land of Carlyle, Lewes and Matthew Arnold. Among recent biographers I should recommend Nevinson for beginners, Robertson for literary criticism, and Hume Brown for the philosophic approach. The most satisfactory German biography is by Bielschowsky, which may be read in a three-volume American translation. Advanced students will naturally turn to the *Transactions of the English Goethe Society*.

Unlike Lessing, his older contemporary, and Schiller, his younger friend, Goethe was born into comfortable circumstances. His autobiography, covering the first twenty-six years of his life, brings us nearer to him than any record or portrait by another hand. Fortunate in most things, he was certainly privileged in the place of his birth. The fine old house at Frankfurt recalls the prosaic father who meant so little to him, and the vivacious mother who meant so much. As one of the so-called Free Cities, Frankfurt was justly proud of its liberties, its wealth, and its past, for it was here that the rulers of the venerable though decrepit Holy Roman Empire were crowned. Situated at the junction of North and South, it was an ideal spot for a man of genius to address his countrymen.

The university years at Leipzig were partially wasted in riotous living; but Goethe soon picked himself up and at Strassbourg he found in Herder his first and only teacher. Destined by his father for the law, he realized in a brief sojourn at Wetzlar that he was made for higher things. Scarcely was he of age than he began to pour forth a stream of novels, poems and plays which set him at the head of the Romantic movement—*The Sorrows of Werther*, which took the world by storm, *Götz*, the most popular of the Storm and Stress dramas before Schiller, the lyrics inspired by Frederike, his first real love, and some scenes of *Faust* which were to lie untouched for many years in his desk.

When Karl August, the young Duke of Weimar, met Goethe at Frankfurt and invited him to live in his little capital, the second period of his life began at the age of twenty-six. That the author of *Werther*, already a celebrity, should be willing for the next ten years to put literature more or less on the shelf and to help his master to govern a tiny Thuringian state, suggests the many-sidedness of his nature. Watching the poet turned Prime Minister we regret the relative sterility of those creative years. But it was not all wasted opportunity or soulless routine. Genius, he declares in the famous lines of *Tasso*, develops in solitude, character in the broad stream of life. The petty principality was a microcosm of the wider world, in which he learned secrets hidden from the pure man of letters—the art of government and the development of the resources of the state. To Herder he was the 'Weimar factotum,' to Knebel 'the backbone of affairs.' While his pen was laid aside, the capable and conscientious official steadily enlarged his basis of induction for an all-embracing philosophy of life.

At the age of thirty-seven, yielding to an irresistible impulse, Goethe jumped into his carriage and drove at top speed towards Italy. The third chapter of his life had opened, and though it only lasted two years its influence, both negative and positive, remained to the end. He turned his back on practical politics, of which he had had his fill, and broke with the Romantic movement, of which he had been a pioneer. In Italy a new world was unfolded before his wondering eyes of which he had read in Winckelmann, a world of classic harmonies in which form replaced emotion and daring flights of imagination were tamed by a discipline self-imposed. In his book, *The Italian Journey*, based on his letters and diaries, we recapture the almost intoxicating delight with which he gazed on the masterpieces of ancient art—a joy that recalls the thrilling excitements of the age of the Renaissance. It was the happiest period of his life.

With his return home in 1788 the fourth period of Goethe's career begins. The life of the little town appeared cold and provincial after the spaciousness of the Eternal City and the genial warmth of an Italian sky. His mind was full of the treasures he had seen, but his artistic rhapsodies fell on deaf ears. For the first time he felt himself a lonely man. His dearest friend Frau von Stein went out of his life and Christiane came in. It was a bad exchange.

The lack of stabilized happiness was in some measure overcome by the friendship with Schiller, which, in Goethe's revealing words, was like a second spring and restored his youth. The most celebrated and fruitful association in the annals of literature should be studied in the correspondence which is one of the heirlooms of the German race. Well might Goethe exclaim in gratitude : ' He gave me back to poetry and life.' For twenty years after the flight to Italy one masterpiece followed another—*Egmont, Tasso, Iphigenie, Wilhelm Meister, Hermann und Dorothea, Elective Affinities*, and the first part of *Faust*.

Meanwhile the French Revolution and the twenty-two years' war which it unleashed brought fresh and dramatic experiences. Goethe accompanied the Duke on the unlucky campaign in France, received his baptism of fire at Valmy, and watched the siege of Mainz in the following year. The Napoleonic era proved even more exciting. He listened to the roar of the guns at Jena, and on the night after the battle his life was threatened by drunken French soldiers who burst into his room. To Goethe, however, Napoleon was not the Corsican ogre but the world-spirit incarnate in a human being. The two greatest personalities of the age met face to face at Erfurt and Weimar, and the Emperor, who had read *Werther* seven times, exclaimed in admiration : *Voilà un homme !*

Meanwhile a fresh sphere of activity had been found in science, which in the middle decades of his life fascinated him no less than literature and art. He had dabbled in medicine and chemistry as a young man at Strassbourg. He loved geology and guessed the significance of fossils. In comparing human and animal skulls in the anatomical department at Jena he came across an important connecting link. ' It is not gold or silver I have found,' he wrote to Herder, ' but something which fills me with unutterable joy. It is the intermaxillary bone in man.' His treatise on *The Metamorphosis of Plants* also pointed towards a theory of evolution, and he claims a place among the forerunners of Darwin. His imposing work on optics, though to some extent love's labour lost, is a monument to his scientific zeal. No one ever approached the study of Nature in a spirit of deeper reverence.

The fifth and last chapter of the long story opens with the return of peace in 1815. Seventeen years of life remained to the man who was now the undisputed monarch of European literature. His heart was still young, and new attachments found expression in lyrics such as he alone could write. His autobiography, the most perfect of his prose writings, reveals the mellow radiance of advancing years, but his creative period was over. The continuation of *Wilhelm Meister* displays a weakening grip, and the second part of *Faust*, completed shortly before his death, is a series of tableaux, not a drama of flesh and blood. The old man rejoiced in the prowess of Byron, but the latest phase of the Romantic Movement for the most part left him cold. As the flame of inspiration died down he became more and more the onlooker—the guide, philosopher, and friend of young men like Thomas Carlyle in search of a compass for stormy seas. The oracle of Weimar lives for ever in the *Conversations with Eckermann*, which ranks with Boswell's *Johnson* among the great books of the world. The end came peacefully in 1832, the year of the Reform Bill. He had warmed both hands before the fire of life. It sank and he was ready to depart.

Now that we have gained some notion of the biographical background, let us return to Goethe's message to the world. A man who took all knowledge, or at any rate all experience, for his province, could hardly be expected to bequeath a system or to found a school. Other makers of the modern spirit whom we are surveying in this series have sounded a clarion call. Goethe's influence has been indirect. It is enshrined in no single work. His legacy is not a creed but an attitude. He was a child of the eighteenth century : but there is always a timeless element in great thinkers, particularly those who strive towards an all-embracing synthesis. Neither a philosopher nor a moralist in the technical sense, he has no rival but Shakespeare in the philosophy of life.

Goethe's religion was equidistant from Christian orthodoxy and the popular eighteenth-century alternative of militant rationalism. In his early years he came under the spell of Spinoza, the most restful of philosophers, the God-intoxicated man, and he remained an idealistic pantheist, or let us say a mystical realist, to the end. ' The finest achievement for a thinker,' he declared, ' is to have fathomed what may be fathomed, and quietly to revere the unfathomable.' He would have agreed with Jeans that science can describe the universe but cannot explain it ; with the argument of Otto that the sense of awe is the root of religion; with Eddington's advice not to tie ourselves up in creeds. Churches and dogmas made no appeal to a mind irradiated by a living sense of the eternal mystery. 'What can our narrow notions tell of the highest Being ? ' he remarked to Eckermann. 'Though I named it with a hundred names I should fall far short. I believe in God and Nature, and the victory of good over evil : but I was also asked to believe that three was one and one was three. That jarred upon my feeling for truth, and I did not see how it could have helped me in the least.'

In the immortal response of Faust to Marguerite's pointed question : 'Believest thou in God ? ' we are listening to Goethe himself. 'Who dares to name Him and to proclaim : I believe ? Who that can feel can bring himself to say : I disbelieve ? The All-embracer, All-sustainer, does He not embrace and sustain thee, me, Himself ? Is not the vault of heaven above and the solid earth beneath ? And do not the everlasting stars shed their friendly light ? Fill thence thy heart. And when thou feelest wholly blest, then call it what thou wilt : Bliss, Heart, Love, God. I have no name for it, 'tis feeling all. Name is but sound and smoke, shrouding the glow of heaven.' It is much the same creedless confession as the testimony of Kant : 'Two things fill me with ever-increasing wonder, the starry heavens above and the moral law within.' No one could say of the two greatest Germans of their time, as Lord Morley has said of Voltaire, that they lacked the sense of holiness. Moreover, Goethe gratefully recognized the supreme and enduring worth of Christian ethics. 'Whatever intellectual progress there may be,' he declared, ' it will never transcend the loftiness of Christianity as it glows and shines in the gospels.'

He might have declared with Spinoza that God reveals Himself in everything, particularly in man, above all in Christ.

Goethe's scientific studies confirmed his instinctive belief in what used to be called Natural Religion. 'In contemplating the structure of the universe,' he remarked, 'we cannot help thinking that an idea underlies the whole, in accordance with which God may work in Nature and Nature in God to all eternity.' No supernatural revelation seemed to him to be needed. The universe was the living garment of God which proclaimed His power and wisdom, working not mechanically but creatively, according to law.

If Goethe learned the doctrine of immanence from Spinoza, his search for the inner purpose in the development of all living things and his joy in the resultant harmony of the whole brings him close to Leibniz. To the quietism of the one he adds the optimism of the other. Convinced of the ultimate rationality of the universe, he believed in some sort of after-life. 'At the age of seventy-five,' he confided to Eckermann, 'one must sometimes think of death, but it never gives me the least uneasiness. For I am convinced that our spirit is indestructible. If I work unceasingly to the end, Nature is bound to provide me with another form of existence when the present can no longer sustain my spirit.'

Goethe was certainly no materialist in religion and philosophy. But did he debase the moral currency by his life and teaching as is sometimes affirmed? He possessed a passionate temperament, and the self-indulgence of his university years revived for a space in middle life. There are lines in the *Roman Elegies* that we should wish away, and if he ever deserved to be called the great pagan it was during his sojourn in Italy. On returning to Weimar, Christiane crossed his path, a bright-faced, healthy girl. Henceforth he had a home. But a mistress is not a wife, and though he married her many years later, she was pathetically unfitted to take her place in social life. Weimar ignored her and she was kept in the background till the end. She inherited from her father a craving for drink, which she transmitted to their son. Thus the man whose range of experience was almost unique never tasted the simple joys of a happy home ; and some people think that it served him right.

Though Goethe's reputation suffered from his domestic embarrassments, he was regarded by his friends with affection and respect. The splendid tribute of Jung Stilling, himself a man of lofty character, will suffice : ' His heart, which few knew, was as great as his intellect, which all knew.' He disliked asceticism in theory and practice, but he was never a cynic or an immoralist. Nietzsche's onslaught on the Christian virtues of compassion and humility would have angered him. He firmly believed in the right and duty of self-realization, and an admirer has spoken of his healthy egotism ; but though he was determined to drain the cup of life he prized the fundamental pieties. He created figures of radiant womanliness— Marguerite and Mignon, Iphigenie and Dorothea, types both of tenderness and strength. ' If you would know for certain what is fitting,' says the Princess in *Tasso*, ' go ask of noble women for the rule.'

No one had a higher conception of the worth of life and the capacities of the human race. ' Let man be noble, helpful and good,' he cries in his magnificent poem, *The Godlike* ; ' for that alone divides him from all beings that we know. Man alone can do the impossible. He chooses and judges. He gives to the moment the duration of eternity.' Goethe speaks of our divinely endowed human nature, and he is convinced of the nobility and the utility of effort. He compares the history of knowledge to a great fugue in which the voices of the nations one after the other emerge. But knowledge has to be related to action, and the culture of which he is the supreme exponent is not by any means purely intellectual. He is delightfully commonplace in his insistence on character and discipline, on the spiritual no less than the practical value of cheerful and well-directed labour. 'An active mind,' he declared, 'keeping with a practical object to the task that lies nearest, is the worthiest thing in the world.' Here and here only, he believed, was the path to happiness and tranquillity of soul, to the development of our personality, to the guiding and preserving of states, to the progress of mankind. Away with vague desires and vain regrets ! There is work to be done and work that we can do. Redemption is the reward of loving service of mankind.

Such is the central gospel of Weimar, presented to us in a thousand forms, in aphorisms and poems, novels and plays. And such, if we take the two parts together, is the message of *Faust*. The dramas of Shakespeare, taken as a whole, present a picture of human life more comprehensive and satisfying than anything in literature ; but *Hamlet*, *Othello*, *King Lear*, are individually only bricks in the stately edifice. *Faust* is unique in the fact that it embodies the moods and meditations of sixty years, that its theme is the education of man, his evolution from youth to old age, from the love-making in the springtime to the governing of men and the making of roads when the end of the journey is in sight. It can never become out of date, for it is the supreme allegory of human life in all its heights and depths. Unlike the *Divina Commedia* and *Paradise Lost*, it is unfettered by the theology of a particular age.

That Goethe was engrossed in the things of the mind, caring little how humbler mortals lived and how the state was governed, is an ignorant calumny. His experience as the colleague and adviser of Karl August supplied him with a philosophy which he retained throughout life. All that he had done and all that he wished to do had been or could be accomplished by the will of a benevolent autocrat. He rejected alike pretentious legitimism and insurgent democracy. The people, he felt, were too uneducated to rule themselves, but they had an unchallengeable right to good government. He was a conservative reformer, convinced that reform must come from above, that changes must be gradual, and that order was Heaven's first law. Though he never expressed his disgust in the passionate tones of Lessing and Schiller, he despised the frivolous despots with whom many of the German states were cursed as heartily as he applauded the efforts of Karl August for the happiness of his subjects. His ideal was expressed in the celebrated aphorism of Frederick the Great—that the ruler is the first servant of the state.

Democracy comes in with the French Revolution, when Goethe's political creed was unalterably fixed; and the decades of confusion that followed were not calculated to commend the new gospel of liberty and equality to a mind set on harmony and discipline. Before the Revolution, he complained, it was all effort; afterwards it was all demand. Yet his attitude towards the Revolution, as embodied in his *Campaign in France*, his political dramas and his conversations, was more understanding than that of Burke. His sympathies with common folk were deep and sincere, and he realized that revolutions are almost invariably the result of misrule. 'When they are due,' he remarked in speaking of the Reformation, ' God is with them and

I

they succeed.' He rightly repudiated the charge that he was a reactionary. ' I am a moderate Liberal, like all sensible men,' he remarked to Eckermann. Personally I should prefer to call him a moderate Conservative. When Karl August, first among German princes, gave Weimar a constitution after the fall of Napoleon, Goethe looked on with misgiving and regret. He had lived into an age of incipient self-determination which he failed to understand. Though sprung from the educated *bourgeoisie*, in which democracy all over the world found its standard-bearers, he was at heart a great aristocrat from beginning to end.

If the eighteenth century was the age of reason, the nineteenth was the era of democracy and nationalism. For the latter Goethe had as little appreciation as for the former. The Free City of Frankfurt he knew, and the Duchy of Weimar, and many another German state ; but there was no Germany before Bismarck. The Wars of Liberation, with their exaltations and agonies, made little appeal to the man who had seen Napoleon. ' How could I write songs of hate without hatred ? ' he remarked many years later. ' Between ourselves I never hated the French, though I was heartily glad to be rid of them. There is a stage where national hatred vanishes altogether, and where one stands to a certain extent above the nations, and feels the weal and woe of a neighbouring people as if it were one's own.' It is the spirit and gospel of Geneva. If Goethe were alive to-day he would acclaim the League of Nations with both hands.

That he failed to realize the strength and the deeper meaning of nationalism is admitted. But we are to-day better able to do justice to his views than our fathers and grandfathers. Nationalism is no more the ultimate solution of the problem of human association than was the cosmopolitanism which it challenged and overthrew. The organization of civilized communities within the boundaries of individual states is the triumph of the last four centuries ; but in achieving it we lost the conception of the unity of civilization, of allegiance to humanity, of a common heritage and a joint responsibility. The cosmopolitans of the eighteenth century, like Goethe, Lessing and Kant, Hume, Gibbon and Voltaire, felt the cultural unity of Europe without realizing the full significance of the national instinct. Schooled by the horrors of the War we are beginning to understand that the greatest task of the twentieth century is the organization of the world. For such an enterprise a synthesis of eighteenth-century cosmopolitanism and nineteenth-century nationalism must be sought and found in a sane internationalism. Of this gospel of corporate consciousness Goethe, like Kant, was a prophet and a pioneer, and he is coming into his own again. Never for a moment did he forget that the supreme concern of us all is the preservation and enrichment of our common civilization. And never has Goethe meant more to his countrymen at home and abroad than in the dark years of defeat and humiliation that followed the World War. Every German held his head a little higher as he remembered that he belonged to the race that had produced the author of *Faust*. Though never a nationalist Goethe had his share in the making of a nation, and to-day he is helping to keep it alive.

A large photograph of Stieler's portrait of Goethe in old age hangs in my library, and I gaze at it with admiration every day of my life. The Olympian intellectuality of that wonderful countenance is unsurpassed. ' His spirit works and searches in all directions,' wrote Schiller, ' and strives to construct a whole—and for me that makes him a great man.'

Matthew Arnold expressed the same idea in his familiar words : ' He saw life steadily and saw it whole.' The richness of his nature, the splendour of his intellect and the range of his experience make his reflections on man and the universe precious to us all. His career is the record of a ceaseless striving towards harmony, passing through the various stages of romanticism and classicism, the governing of a state and the exploration of the physical world, the love of women and the society of men, the joys of travel and the tragedies of war. When I think of Goethe I see the vision and promise of the universal man. I dream of widening horizons, the breaking down of barriers between religion and science, the co-operation of the nations, the cult of beauty, the unresting march of the human spirit, the fashioning of a richer life.

## IX

## JEREMY BENTHAM

## (1748—1832)

### By W. Ivor Jennings

I DON'T know if others have the same feeling, but to me the great figures of history do not become real until I reach the 'thirties of last century. When I think of the Cabinet of 1841, in which Sir Robert Peel was Prime Minister and Mr. Gladstone among the other ministers, I think of men whose ways I understand. But when my mind travels back beyond 1832 I come into a world in which the personalities appear almost alien. But curiously enough, I make an exception of Jeremy Bentham. For though he was born in 1748 and died three days before the Reform Act became law in 1832, I feel that he belongs not to the eighteenth century but to the nineteenth century. Indeed, in a sense he was the embodiment of the spirit of nineteenth-century England. For his ideas dominated most of the political and social changes which took place until the very end of the century. He had nineteenth-century ideas in eighteenth-century surroundings.

To explain to you why Bentham had such an influence upon the modern mind I must tell you something of Jeremy himself. He was born in 1748, the son of an ambitious and wealthy attorney, or solicitor. And let me tell you at once that at no time did Bentham work for his living. He was never very rich, but he had income enough to write for posterity and not for profit. People who work for their living cannot afford to sap the foundations of contemporary society as Bentham did. Jeremy's grandfather had also been an attorney and he himself was destined for the legal profession. Indeed, his father hoped that such a precocious youth would obtain some of those glittering prizes of wealth and social position to which success at the Bar has always led. Of his precocity there can be no doubt. He knew his letters before he could talk, and at the age of three he preferred to read Rapin's *History of England* rather than go for a walk with his parents. He went to Oxford at the age of twelve, and took his degree three years later. In 1763, therefore, he was ready to begin his study of the law.

The period during which Bentham thought and wrote may therefore be said to extend from about 1760 to 1832. Now these dates are important, because they correspond roughly with that great period of economic and social development which is called the Industrial Revolution. Water power first, and then steam power, revolutionized industry and shifted the balance of the population. The great inventions of this period and the development of the means of transport produced the factory system, while agricultural changes made less important the economic position of the landowner. To put the change in a sentence, the power of the fox-hunting squire in the county was balanced by the power of the factory owner in the towns. The towns sprang up like mushrooms, and the new industrial middle class dominated them as the squire dominated the country. The difference was that anybody could become a capitalist by luck or knavery or hard work, whereas one had to buy an estate and be accepted by 'the county' as a 'gentleman' to become a squire.

Also, in the earlier part of the Industrial Revolution there happened an event which shook the world out of its lethargy. The French Revolution of 1789 had no parallel in England. In fact its immediate effect was to enable the reactionary elements in the English governing class to submerge most of the liberal elements. The liberal Burke became a raging Tory in all but name. Political unorthodoxy was ruthlessly attacked by all Governments from 1789 to 1830. But the consequences of great events are not so easily disposed of. The Revolution set new ideas in motion, and the growing population of the towns, having no roots in the soil, accepted them eagerly. The economic changes of the Industrial Revolution and the new ideas released by the French Revolution prepared the way for the nineteenth-century mind which Bentham was to do so much to create.

But I should mislead you if I caused you to think that Bentham was in his early days either a revolutionary or a radical. Revolutionary he never was, though he was made a citizen of the French Republic, and it was only towards the end of the century that he would have admitted that he was a radical. In his youth he was a Tory, and he disliked the ideas of Rousseau and of the other philosophers of the French Revolution. He began his writing as a critic of the law, and only in the second half of his life did he begin to attack political institutions as well as the law of England.

Let us go back, then, to 1763, when Bentham began to study the law. Until 1758, the only way to learn the law was to attend the courts, and to read the ancient law books, especially those of Coke, the Chief Justice who, in the words of Carlyle, 'shovelled up his enormous learning in vast disorderly heaps.' But in 1758 one William Blackstone began teaching English law in the University of Oxford. In order to listen to his lectures Bentham went back to Oxford for a few months. Now the law at this time was a chaos of obsolete, inconsistent and frequently unjust rules. It had been developed by the judges around a mass of ancient remedies. Its forms and ceremonies had become all-important, and nobody considered whether it was good law or bad. Blackstone, like most lawyers, had enormous veneration for its forms and ceremonies. He was what is called a 'sound lawyer.' That is, he knew all the statutes and all the precedents, and had read widely in the ancient books of authority. But he differed from most lawyers in that he had an excellent literary style. And it is because he was a sound lawyer who, as Bentham put it, first made English law speak the language of the scholar and the gentleman, that he has acquired such a great reputation among lawyers. But he was nothing more. He had no originality : he was incapable of thinking out any of the more fundamental problems underlying the law.

Yet in order to expound English law, Blackstone had to discuss these problems. He had to say something of the nature of the state, of the theory of law, of the relations between the law and the state. Having no ideas of his own, he naturally took them from other people. He gave a synthesis of the political theory of the late seventeenth and early eighteenth century. But he was quite out of his depth. For political theory demands more than mere book-learning : it demands capacity for individual thought. And of this Blackstone had very little. Naturally, therefore, his treatment of such important subjects did not meet with the approval of a mind so precise and so unorthodox

as that of Bentham. He tells us that he immediately
detected the fallacy in one of Blackstone's doctrines.
Another he thought ' frivolous and illogical.'

The result was that when Bentham went back to
London to study law, he was more interested in reading
the political and moral philosophy that Blackstone
did not understand than the law books in which
Blackstone was deeply read, and in which Bentham
ought to have made himself proficient if he was to
succeed at the Bar. Bentham did study the law, but
with fundamental principles in his mind which were
quite inconsistent with the strange mass of rules that he
found the law of England to be. He became not a
lawyer, but a law-reformer. He tells us that he wanted
to become ' the Newton of legislation ' ; he wanted to
think out scientifically the principles of law-making.
He was called to the Bar in 1769, but to the intense
disgust of his father he advised his first client that
litigation would only benefit the attorneys, and that
he ought to settle the case out of court. That, as his
father knew, was not the way to the House of Lords.
Successful lawyers fought their cases until all the money
at stake had been transferred from their clients' pockets
to their own.

He had indeed decided that practice in the legal
profession was not to be his career. He had discovered
what he believed to be the fundamental principle for
law-making. Laws must be so made, he said, as to
produce *the greatest happiness of the greatest number*. He
called this ' the principle of utility.' And he was
trying to work out what this meant, and how it was
to be applied to the reform of the law. ' Nature
has placed mankind,' he explained, ' under the
governance of two sovereign masters, pain and pleasure.' This meant that from the point of view of the
individual another's action was good or bad according

as it produced pleasure or pain. Since a community is built up of individuals, an action on behalf of the community ought to produce the greatest possible amount of happiness in the greatest possible number of individuals.

I don't want to discuss with you the adequacy of this philosophy. I am concerned with its effects, not with its value. I must discuss, therefore, only those aspects of it which have influenced—and immensely influenced—the development of the modern mind.

The first point to which I wish to draw your attention is that it does provide a test of value. An institution is not justified merely by its existence: it must be shown to have some utility in the wide sense in which Bentham used that term. If it has not, it must be swept away. Any rule of law, for instance, is bad unless it can be shown to have some utility. Lawyers frequently speak of a judicial decision as being ' good law.' But they don't mean by that that it is good in its consequences, that it provides justice, or in some other way conduces to human happiness. They mean only that it is consistent with the precedents. It is good law not because there is any reason for it, but because it is true to history ; and history, as Bentham said, is not a reason. Now, whether Bentham's test is a good one or a bad one you will agree with me, won't you, that there ought to be some test of the value of the law ? The proof of the pudding is in the eating, not in the making. But lawyers are always making puddings for other people to eat, and they never consider whether they are edible.

But you will see, and this is my second point, that such a method of criticism is not limited to the law. It can be applied to the whole range of human institutions. Bentham began as a lawyer, but soon found himself led to criticize all the major political and social institutions of his time. Could the then House of Commons or the House of Lords or the monarchy be justified ? Was there any utility in colonies ? Was international war consistent with the principles of utility? Was there justification for the poor law system, corrupt municipalities, monopolies, the limitation of educational facilities to the rich, the laws against usury, the laws which restricted freedom of trade, secret diplomacy ? All these questions demanded answers as soon as the principle of utility was established. For human institutions need to be justified, and they can be justified only on the basis of a philosophy.

Here again there is a lesson to be learned. For we are suffering from what I may call the tyranny of the expert. The lawyer tells us that certain things must not be done because they conflict with the principles of the common law. The economist tells us that certain other things must not be done because they conflict with the principles which his science has developed. The politician tells us that certain things must not be done because they conflict with the ' rights ' of certain sections of the population. But really, whether any of the things ought to be done depends, as Bentham has shown us, upon the value of their consequences. And until the expert tells us by what principle he tests values, he has no right to express any opinion to which we need pay attention. An economist, for instance, cannot tell us whether tariffs, or the tenets of socialism, are bad unless he tells us what are the principles upon which he determines what is good and what is evil ; and these principles we are as capable of finding out as he is. It is not for the expert to tell us what to do ; it is for us to tell the expert what we want done.

The third point to which I want to draw your attention doesn't appear on the face of the principle of utility. That principle depends upon the happiness of the individual, upon the presence of pleasure and the absence of pain. Now, what is pleasure and what is pain? Bentham investigated this at great length. But he admitted that in the last resort the individual was the only person who could judge of his own happiness. Consequently, though he must be restrained from injuring others, he must be left as much as possible to find his happiness in his own way. Any legal restriction which prevented him from doing so was therefore an evil in itself. In other words, Bentham supported, though he did not originate, the doctrine of *laisser-faire*. His argument led him to recommend the sweeping away of all the restrictions which prevented industry from developing in its own way.

This point is important, because it led to results which were demanded of the manufacturer in his own interest. The Industrial Revolution produced numbers of middle-class capitalists who found their enterprise restricted on every side by laws as to wages, apprenticeship, prices and import and export duties. They wanted freedom from every sort of state control, freedom to take profit wherever and however it could be found. Now, by the Reform Act this class received the right to vote. Consequently, it became politically as well as economically the dominating class of the community. This is one explanation of the remarkable influence of Bentham's ideas in the nineteenth century. At the same time, it was in this direction that Bentham's influence came to an end most quickly. For when later Reform Acts, in accordance with Bentham's proposals, gave the political predominance to the working class, the leading idea quickly changed. Members of the working class did not consider that the freedom of the middle class to take profit necessarily inured to their benefit. In their view their interests demanded restrictions. They demanded, too, that the state should provide essential services in order that they might not be exploited by the middle class. Consequently, all political parties since 1867 have become more or less socialist. They have recognized an obligation to intervene actively in the conduct of industry and commerce in order to provide an equitable distribution of the product ; and they have differed only about what was equitable and about the method of achieving it. In particular, the radical movement which was inspired by Bentham's ideas gradually accepted Socialist ideas. John Stuart Mill, the greatest of the followers of Bentham, was already veering towards socialism in the 'sixties. By the 'eighties the left wing of the Liberal party was definitely socialist ; and by the end of the century there was growing up a body of men who frankly called themselves socialists. In this field, therefore, Bentham's ideas have in practice been superseded.

The last element of the principle of utility which I will mention is its emphasis upon equality. The happiness of one person cannot be more important than the happiness of another. Bentham did not say that all men were born equal. He would have said that such a statement was ' nonsense upon stilts.' His idea of equality was that of equality of opportunity. It was this which made Bentham a radical. For he was compelled to attack all forms of privilege, and the eighteenth century was built up upon privilege. He was compelled to demand universal manhood suffrage (and John Stuart Mill went to the logical conclusion and demanded the vote for women too). And since every man must learn how to seek his own happiness, Bentham demanded universal education.

This, then, was the principle of utility. Bentham began rapidly, almost feverishly, to work out its consequences in all branches of human activity. In University College, London, there are eighty boxes of his manuscripts. Some of them were published by Bentham. Others were published by his disciples in his lifetime. One of his disciples, Bowring, published a collected edition after Bentham's death in eleven enormous volumes. But there is still much unpublished. And one of the things which the University of London would like to do is to publish a really well-edited collection. To explain all that he wrote about, and to attempt to assess the influence which he had upon the great reform movements of the nineteenth century, would occupy a book. For in the field of social institutions there was no limit to the range of his interests. Let me take, therefore, the most significant of his contributions to practical reform.

The principle of utility, as I have already explained, grew out of his interest in law reform. In the law of the eighteenth century the medieval jostled the Georgian, and the feudal system rubbed shoulders with the Reformation. The rules satisfied no intelligible principle, but depended upon artificial concepts established by medieval judges and elaborated by their successors. Law reform began even before the passing of the Reform Bill. There was, for example, a wonderful six-hour speech by Henry Brougham, based upon Benthamite ideas, which forecast the great changes which were necessary in legal procedure. Sir Robert Peel, too, did something to amend the criminal law. After 1832 the movement gathered strength, and much was done to make the law more accessible, more intelligible, and more reasonable. The county courts were established in 1846, chiefly through the insistence of Brougham. The central courts were partly reformed in 1873. But the fundamental reform which Bentham advocated has never been brought about. He contended, and in my opinion contended rightly, that law could be made simple, accessible, intelligible and just if it were enacted in a single statute, called a *Code*. English law is in fact the most complicated in the world. It is quite inaccessible to those who have not the right of entry to a law library. A complete set of the necessary books would cost some thousands of pounds. And even when access is obtained, the material cannot be understood except by those who have spent long hours in trying to master its complications. It is contained in some four thousand statutes, some of them in a language which nobody has spoken for five hundred years, and in thousands of decisions rendered by all sorts of judges, good and bad, since medieval times. Above all, nobody except Bentham has ever sat down to consider seriously what the rules of law ought to be. Like Topsy, they have ' just growed,' and whether they are good or bad, they are the law of England.

On the political side reforms came more slowly, but have proceeded further. For the great radical movement which Bentham and his disciples originated has always been represented in Parliament, while law reformers there have been few. Every adult now has the right to vote, though it was not accorded until 1928. The reformed Parliament itself reformed the poor law along Benthamite lines, and did a little to reform the municipal corporations. Bentham's disciples, aided by an epidemic of cholera and the disgusting state of the mushroom towns, induced Parliament to establish the modern system of public health and so paved the way to the great development of local government. In some respects the Local Government Act of 1929 carried out his ideas. The ballot is now prescribed for nearly all

elections.  But the House of Lords remains unreformed
and there is much in local government that needs
alteration.

His immediate influence upon international affairs
was small.  But in the twenty-four pages of his *Principles of International Law* you will find many of the
post-War developments recommended.  He wanted
disarmament, and argued that unilateral disarmament
was to the advantage of Great Britain.  He wanted the
codification of international law so that everybody
might know when a state was the aggressor.  He
wanted an international court of justice to determine
disputes between states, though without coercive
powers.  He wanted a sort of international legislature
which looks surprisingly like the League of Nations.
And he wanted open diplomacy and the publication of
treaties.  I think you will agree with me that such
proposals, written nearly one hundred and thirty years
before the outbreak of the Great War, show an admirable
appreciation of the problems of international peace.
And perhaps if all the nations had accepted his advice
and had refused to lay claim to any more colonies there
would have been no Great War at all.  For whatever
the immediate causes of that war might have been it
is now commonly accepted that its ultimate origin was
the development of imperialism in all countries after
1850.

I can mention some only of his other proposals.  We
now have universal elementary education, as he recommended, and the way is open to any child of unusual
ability to proceed to a university, no matter how poor
his parents.  The way is made less difficult than it
would be through the establishment of the modern
universities ; and those universities have followed many
of the ideals, such as the adequate study of natural
science and of law, politics and economics, the

admission of all persons without reference to wealth or social position, and freedom from all religious tests, which Bentham insisted should be the characteristic of the University of London, which he helped to found.

But above all what he did was to establish one fundamental principle. Social and political institutions must justify themselves. Privileges based upon wealth, or ancestry, or past depredations, must be swept away. Human actions and human organizations must be submitted to the test of reason. If they fail to pass that test and defend themselves by reference to history, the time has come for them to be swept away. That is the essence of the Benthamite position. It represents Bentham's greatest contribution to the modern mind. We talk of ' our country,' of patriotism, of rights, of liberty, and of a host of other things which we leave undefined and uncriticized. We allow ourselves to be led away by words and emotions. Bentham showed us that there is only one test of values, and that is reason.

X

# CHARLES DARWIN

## (1809—1882)

### By Doris L. Mackinnon, D.Sc.

*Professor of Zoology, University of London, King's College*

I HOPE to show you what was the extraordinary
influence that Charles Darwin exercised, not only
on the science of biology but on the development
of what we call the modern spirit generally. Acceptance of the doctrine of organic evolution marked an
epoch ; and every educated person to-day has some
notion of what the *Origin of Species* was about.

But often these notions are vague or distorted.
Perhaps you know the story of the schoolboy who was
told to write an essay on evolution, and handed in a
single sheet on which was written : ' Mr. Darwin said
that the first monkey was a kind of a jelly.' Of course,
Mr. Darwin said nothing of the sort ; nor was he
directly responsible for the amoeba-to-man crudities
of our text-books and newspapers. And he would be
scandalized if he knew how his theory of natural
selection has been used to justify much that is worst in
our modern civilization.

There was nothing of the red revolutionary about
Darwin himself. He was a tolerant English gentleman,
with a good sense of humour, and rather unusually

sensitive where other people's prejudices were concerned. He came of solid *bourgeois* stock. His
mother was a daughter of Josiah Wedgwood. His
father, Robert Darwin, was a highly successful family
doctor in Shrewsbury. His grandfather, Erasmus
Darwin, had also been a doctor. And Charles himself
would have followed in the family tradition, but that
the sight of blood always turned him sick and faint ;
so he left Edinburgh University after he had been a
medical student there only two years. That was in
1828, when he was not yet nineteen. From Edinburgh
he went to Cambridge. As he was not fitted to be a
doctor, they thought he might as well become a clergy-
man. He says himself that, so far as his academic
studies were concerned, his time at Cambridge was as
much wasted as at school in Shrewsbury or at the
University of Edinburgh. He distinguished himself
in no way—not even in sport. He was strong and
active rather than athletic. He was an excellent shot ;
but later in life he gave this up, for he conceived a great
horror of killing creatures unnecessarily. At Cambridge, however, as already at Edinburgh, natural
history was his real interest (even as a schoolboy he
had assiduously collected beetles), and he made his
friends among the naturalists—men, for the most part,
much older than himself. In talk with them, rather
than from their lectures, he learnt what they could
teach him. After he took a very undistinguished
degree in 1831, he remained at Cambridge studying
geology for two more terms ; and those, at least, were
very profitably spent. But you could hardly imagine
a greater contrast at this stage than between those two
young Cambridge graduates, Newton and Darwin—
the one already mature and making his great scientific
discoveries, the other still just a rather diffident and not
too promising lad.

And now it is necessary to inquire what were the opinions that this seemingly docile youth accepted from those who taught him and talked with him at Cambridge—opinions which he was so dramatically to challenge thirty years later.  In the eighteen-thirties it was still very generally believed that all the various kinds of animals and plants upon this earth are the direct descendants of organisms just like themselves, which had been specially created ' in the beginning.' If you were puzzled to find fossil in the rocks the remains of animals and plants unlike any that now live, you were told that perhaps there had been a series of catastrophes in the course of the earth's history—floods such as Noah's, or possibly great volcanic eruptions— which had so far denuded the world of its inhabitants that further acts of creation had been necessitated from time to time.  Most men held such views.  But there were exceptions.  There were a few who believed that there is a gradual change from generation to generation as time goes on, and that the species of living beings as we see them now have been slowly developed from— have *evolved* from—others that were different and in the main simpler, many of them long extinct.  This idea of an organic evolution is very old.  If it is not as old as the hills, it is, in a rather special sense, at least as old as the Greeks.  But the people who took it seriously were, for the most part, poets or cranks.  Goethe undoubtedly was an evolutionist ; but scientific specialists always tend to discount the opinions of the many-sided genius, especially if he be an artist. . . .  You might have supposed, however, that they would have taken more heed of what the great French naturalist, Lamarck, had to say, since no one could accuse *him* of making science his mere hobby.  In Lamarck's *Philosophie Zoologique*, first published in 1809—the year in which Charles Darwin was born—the case for evolution was put for the first time with exactness and force ; and Lamarck even went so far as to suggest a method whereby evolution may have come about. But just then it happened that biologists were completely under the domination of the famous anatomist, Cuvier. Now Cuvier disapproved of Lamarck ; so, with the habitual snobbishness of lesser men, his scientific brethren agreed also to disapprove. And Lamarck was treated as a joke.

But Charles Darwin had better reason than most of his contemporaries at Cambridge to know something of the evolutionary heresy. His own grandfather, the eccentric old doctor, Erasmus Darwin, had relieved the tedium of his daily rounds by writing several queer books, sometimes in verse : and with one of these, *Zoonomia*, Charles became early acquainted. In *Zoonomia* Dr. Erasmus Darwin expressed himself a convinced evolutionist before Lamarck, for the work was published in 1794.

Now, I have had to say all this because far too often people speak as though Charles Darwin was the originator of the theory of organic evolution. . . . I'll come back to that point presently. For the moment, let us see what the boy did when he left Cambridge. Apparently he had given up all idea of entering the Church. It was not at all clear what he *should* do. And while he was trying to make some plan, the great chance of his life came along. H.M.S. *Beagle* was sailing for the Pacific on a five years' surveying cruise, and they wanted a naturalist on board. Darwin applied for the job. His qualifications were considered good enough, but he nearly didn't get it because FitzRoy, the commander of the *Beagle*, didn't like the shape of his nose. FitzRoy was an ardent disciple of Lavater, the physiognomist, and at a time when all England was still overshadowed by the Duke of Wellington's profile,

Charles Darwin's nose may have seemed inadequate for one from whom so much energy and determination would be required. Still, it was a better nose than Socrates'; and perhaps Captain FitzRoy found compensations in the eyes and forehead. Anyhow, he took Darwin along with him on the *Beagle*. And among the books that Darwin took to sea were *Paradise Lost* and the newly published *Principles of Geology*, in which Charles Lyell showed that there is no good evidence for theories of catastrophism and that the fossil-bearing rocks succeed one another in an orderly series.

And now for five years the young naturalist was left entirely on his own to observe what he could of the inhabitants, both plant and animal, both dead and living, of the strange lands the *Beagle* visited, and to record as best he could what he observed, and to speculate uninfluenced concerning the origins of what he saw.

Here I would emphasize the fact that, amateurish though his training may have been, Darwin was an all-round naturalist in the way that few men are now : he was a botanist and a geologist at least as much as he was a zoologist. He saw the face of Nature whole. But unlike most men of his time, he saw also that it was the face of a sphinx ; he saw very early that there was a riddle to be guessed, and already on the *Beagle* he set himself to guess the riddle. . . . When Darwin was a young man, biologists were almost all given over to collecting facts ; theorizing was considered dangerous and it was sternly discouraged. And it *is* dangerous, unless the theorist—the man gifted with imagination—also has the determination to test his theories at every point by appeal to the world of facts. What distinguishes Darwin so especially among scientific men is the power he had of accumulating and marshalling facts on the one hand, and, on the other, of forming bold hypotheses which might make these facts intelligible as parts of a greater whole. And he was always utterly without the petty vanity that causes a man to be tenacious of a cherished opinion against the evidence.

I will now give you an example of the form in which the great riddle presented itself to Darwin when he was on the *Beagle*. In the course of the voyage, they came to the Galapagos archipelago, a group of about a dozen rocky, volcanic islands right on the equator, about 500 miles west of South America, and separated by deep and wide channels through which the currents run swiftly. They are, in fact, quite isolated from the mainland and from one another, and perhaps they have been thus isolated for millions of years. Darwin found no native mammals on the Galapagos Islands ; and that seemed odd. He saw the giant tortoises described by earlier visitors—tortoises measuring as much as three feet in length—and such as elsewhere are known only as fossils. He also found quantities of enormous lizards, and among them, living on seaweed, the only marine lizard in the world. And there were many other peculiar animals. But a more subtle sort of strangeness about the fauna was this— that when he compared the islands one with another, he found that each had its own peculiar species of the larger groups common to all and to the mainland 500 miles away. The mocking-thrush of Charles Island, for instance, was different from the mocking-thrush of Chatham Island, and both of these were different from the mocking-thrush of Albemarle Island. Could it really be true that, in the beginning, Nature had invented all these different species, one for each island, and had set them down there to live each in its appointed place, unchanged and unchanging, from the creation until 1835 ? Or was it possible that ' in the long course of time the individuals of the same species, and likewise allied species, have proceeded from some one source ? ' For, if this is so, ' all the grand leading facts of geographical distribution are explicable on the theory of migration together with subsequent modifications and the multiplication of new forms.'

In the last sentences I was quoting Darwin himself. But those words were not written until long after he had returned from his voyage, and not until he had pondered for twenty years on what he had seen then and on the other sorts of evidence for organic evolution which he laboriously collected between 1836 and his first sketch of the *Origin of Species*.

With his return to England ended all Darwin's active life—if by that one means his travels and adventures. He never left England again, and he seldom went far from the country house of Down in Kent which he bought a few years after his happy marriage to his cousin Emma Wedgwood in 1839. Through the generosity of Sir Buckston Browne, Down was recently purchased and endowed as a memorial to Darwin ; and any one may visit it and see just what were the peaceful surroundings in which he worked as a recluse until his death in 1882. The seclusion of his life was not of Darwin's own choosing, for by nature he was sociable and a most charming guest and host. It was necessitated by illness. He was never the same man after he came back from the voyage on the *Beagle*. His son Francis says of him that for forty years he was never a day without pain, and he had to stick very closely to the only routine of living that made it possible to carry on his innumerable experiments and to write his epoch-making books.

In 1844 he says in one of his letters : ' I am almost convinced that species are not immutable.' And he adds : ' It is like confessing a murder.' By every approach that he made to the sphinx's riddle he was getting the same answer. The evidences came from five directions—or, to quote Darwin's own words, from ' the general facts in the affinities, embryology, rudimentary organs, geological history and geographical distribution of organic species.' The evidence from any one direction could not be regarded as conclusive in itself; but, taken together, they gave such strong support to the evolutionary hypothesis that there seemed no escape from accepting the explanation it offered of facts irreconcilable with theories of special creation.

But Darwin did not rest satisfied. He next set about trying to formulate his ' notions on the *means* by which Nature makes her species.' And by 1858 he had arrived at his theory of Natural Selection. Many were the influences that directed him to his conclusions. I shall mention but two. In 1838 he had read Malthus's *On Population*, and had been deeply impressed by that book's revelation of the competition for the necessities of life that goes on between members of an increasing population. And then he had also studied at first-hand how the breeder of domestic animals and plants proceeds when he wishes to obtain a new variety. No two puppies in a litter, no two plants from the one batch of seed are alike. There is, as we say, variation, even among closely related animals or plants of the same species. Moreover, variations tend to be inherited. And, if the dog fancier wants a new variety of dog, he picks out from the litter the animals that show most markedly the character he wishes emphasized. And from this stock alone does he breed, selecting again at every birth and mating still with an eye to the new type; and with time and patience he gets his St. Bernard or his Pekinese. That, put very diagrammatically, is ' artificial selection.' Now, thought

Darwin, may it not be that something of the same sort is going on in conditions more natural than the kennel or the dovecot ? Is it not possible that in competition with their too numerous relatives for food and mates, and in competition with organisms of other kinds also, and in their fight against the elements themselves, those individuals of a species will be the ones that on the whole tend to survive and mate and reproduce their kind which have characters that render them a little stronger, or fleeter, or more cunning, or more immune to disease, than their fellows ? And if this goes on for untold thousands of years, will you not in the end find creatures, perhaps in a changed environment, that have come to be so different from their remote ancestors in respect of certain characters that the classifier would place them in a different species ? This, then, again put very diagrammatically, was Darwin's theory of Natural Selection to account for organic evolution—to account, that is to say, for the slow changing of one species into another in the course of time. And the theory of natural selection is Darwin's really original contribution to the development of the evolutionary hypothesis.

Yet he was not alone to have the idea. Just as Newton's great principles were on the verge of being discovered by other men when he came along, so now with Darwin. Organic evolution and natural selection were in the air, so to speak. As Darwin was putting the finishing touches to the *Origin of Species*, he was dismayed to receive for criticism a manuscript from a young man called Alfred Russel Wallace ; and in that manuscript he saw himself forestalled. Wallace had approached the problem from a somewhat different angle, but he had come to the same general conclusions ; and it is to Wallace that we owe the phrase : ' the struggle for existence.' It was characteristic of

Darwin's generosity that he at once decided to let the younger man have full credit for his discovery ; and together they read a paper before the Linnean Society in 1858.

But when at last *The Origin of Species by means of Natural Selection* was published in 1859, public attention was turned on Darwin and on Darwin alone. The first edition of the book was exhausted on the day of its appearance. Its popularity increased. It became a best seller. It appealed to the man of science because, as I have indicated, it gave prime place to an eminently reasonable explanation of the method whereby evolution may have come about. And with the general public the *Origin* caught on, partly because it was written without pedantry and in such a way that any educated man who chose to use his brains could follow the line of argument. But undoubtedly its success was also a *succès de scandale*. If you want to capture a man's attention, there is nothing like a taunt. It is true that the *Origin of Species* makes little direct reference to the origin of man, and Darwin did not publish *The Descent of Man* for another twelve years. But the implication was obvious. Man was one with the rest of the animal creation, and lower than the angels by several more degrees than he had been led to suppose. . . . Moreover, since it became clear that the process of evolution could not have been gone through in so short a time as 4,000 years, and since the forms of organic life that first inhabited the earth must have been vastly different from those we now see, the account given in the first book of the Bible could no longer be taken literally by those who would be evolutionists. Furthermore—and this is very important—it was evident that natural law must operate in the world of living things as surely as in the world of the purely physical. Now, while the doctrine of evolution itself seems no offence to deism, the theory of natural selection is definitely mechanistic. If one accepted it, a mechanistic conception of human progress appeared inevitable ; and for many people that is sheer irreligion.

But it is difficult seventy years after the event to realize how great the scandal seemed, and how bitter was the resistance by the old culture to this further invasion of the sanctuary. Tolerant agnostic that he was, Darwin was much distressed by the religious controversy that his scientific honesty had excited, and by the unpleasant notoriety it brought on him. Averse to public appearance and debate, he remained quietly in his study at Down and left Thomas Huxley to battle with the bishops.

And in an amazingly short space of time—for men's minds had long been getting ready to receive it—the doctrine of organic evolution was very generally accepted, and another breach—a very wide one, this— was made in the crumbling fortifications of the old culture. The effect on biological science of a unifying principle was instant and far-reaching, and there followed a period of immense activity and productiveness. Geology, physics and chemistry all benefited, for to have biology come into line with her sister sciences greatly strengthened the whole scientific position. New sciences sprang up ; for, properly speaking, there were no sciences of anthropology or sociology before Darwin's time, and since his day psychology has ceased to be a mere inquisitiveness concerning mental disorders and is becoming a science which holds untold potentialities for the future. With psychological science all modern systems of education are bound up. The study of history took on a new aspect. The study of languages became a science. Finally, the conception of evolution had a profound influence on modern philosophy—as you shall hear in a later chapter.

And the layman, too, recovering from the first shock to his vanity, began to appreciate the new freedom from traditional trammels to thought that acceptance of the evolutionary theory brought with it. And he began to see the great and inspiring hope for the human race that the doctrine of evolution holds out. For if it be true that the apes are our relations, still they are very poor relations, whom mentally we have incredibly transcended in what, geologically speaking, is a very short space of time. And we are only at the beginning. There are millions of years before us wherein our race may still have time and opportunity to work out its great destiny. May it not be that man, as we see him now, is but a shadow of the god-like image into which he may yet be fashioned ?

Literal acceptance of the theory of natural selection, however, as the means whereby organic evolution may have come to pass—that is another question. Natural selection was taken up with enthusiasm by Darwin's followers among the scientists, and it was pressed into the service of explaining many things to which probably Darwin himself would never have applied it. Absurdities have arisen, and of recent years there has been some reaction. Especially since the sciences of palaeontology, genetics and ecology have brought to light facts unknown in Darwin's day, there has been some scepticism as to whether things can really have worked out just in the way he supposed. Whether, for instance, the slight, continuous variations with which Darwin was concerned really can give to organisms so much advantage over their fellows as to ensure survival.

Now, whether the biologist's questionings are justified or not, certain it seems to be that a crude application of the theory of natural selection to a complicated modern human society makes for absurdities—and worse. Control over his environment has put civilized man in a very different position from other animals. Civilized man is artificially protected by the tools he has devised, by the resources of medicine, by the inheritance of social position and wealth, in such a way as to remove him far from Nature and to make it difficult for selection to work effectively on him as possibly it may work on creatures nakedly exposed to their elemental environment. Consider Darwin's own case. If *he* had had to struggle for his existence in fierce competition with other men, he would probably not have survived long after thirty, since he was physically so far from fit. He was protected by human artifice—by his inherited wealth and by the régime imposed on him by modern medicine. Yet if this physically unfit man had not survived through his productive years, development of what we call the modern spirit would have been far slower than we know it to have been. I raise this protest against wholesale application of the natural selection slogans— ' struggle for existence ' and ' survival of the fittest ' (neither of them Darwin's phrases, by the way—one was Wallace's and the other Herbert Spencer's). I raise this protest because they are too often used to justify the oppression of the poor by the rich, of the weak by the strong, and as the great justification for war. Even after our recent experiences there are plenty of people who regard war as a justifiable form of struggle for existence in modern society, since it is ' natural,' they say, and must therefore determine by law the survival of the fittest. Whereas while *pugnacity* may be natural, we all know perfectly well that, under modern conditions, what *war* results in is merely the momentary triumph of the richer nation, and the survival within both combatant nations of the feeblest and the oldest male stock.

Professor Macmurray tells us in his essay that the Great War brought to an end the second stage of modern development—the stage of naturalism. In the course of the naturalistic phase men came to depend more and more on the guidance of science in the affairs of life. Perhaps, since it seems that science has let us down so badly, we are now seeking for some other help. But to have interested men in their origin as well as in their destiny, to have given them an aesthetically satisfying view of Nature as a whole, and to have forced them to consider themselves more and more in relation to other organisms—these are not small contributions from science to the art of living ; and it was Charles Darwin who made them.

## XI

## NIETZSCHE

## (1844—1900)

### By GEOFFREY SAINSBURY

THE theory of evolution is a convenient point of departure when we come to study Nietzsche's philosophy. *The Origin of Species*, the book which did more than any other to spread the theory of evolution, was published when Nietzsche was fifteen. I do not know when Nietzsche came to know it, but evolution must have been the subject of widespread discussion in his student days. Nietzsche's contribution to the subject may roughly be described in this way : the evolutionists were concerned with the actual development of man from some simpler organic form. Nietzsche was concerned to write the ethical commentary on their work. If man was an animal, what were we to think of his ' animal ' nature, his so-called ' lower ' nature ? If man were an animal, had we any further right to use the word animal as a term of reproach ? We hardly had ; so man's animal nature stood forthwith justified. And what about his ' higher ' nature, the spiritual man ? If man was an animal, all that we had called his spiritual nature fell also within the animal world. Thus the distinction between soul and body disappeared. But this brought all man's virtues and vices on to a common footing. Was that ' evil ' ?

In the Christian confession man had to produce the right answers to his inward questions—the good answers. But then the question came: Are those good answers, those virtuous answers, true? Are not the ' right ' answers rather the true ones? To question the rightness of the ' good ' answers—was that evil? No, it was just investigation, it was just *beyond good and evil*.

It is in some ways unfortunate that this phrase was ever formulated. For it has enabled people to think that Nietzsche was the enemy of all moral values. Nothing could be further from the truth. Nietzsche was a moralist from first to last ; indeed, his moral fervour cannot be stressed too strongly. Because he attacked Christianity he has often been popularly regarded, particularly in England, as the instinctively immoral man inventing a new morality to justify himself, as the ' big blond beast ' setting up an image of himself to justify his cruel and predatory nature. A variant of the same view has sometimes shown itself among his nominal adherents—those who like to kick over the traces, repudiate all restraint, and make Nietzsche the patron saint of what Americans call ' whoopee.' Such views are a complete misreading of Nietzsche's character and work. ' We are not born,' he wrote in one of his letters, ' to be happy, but to do our duty, and we can be thankful when we know where our duty lies.' Nothing was more contemptible in his eyes than the pursuit of happiness. ' Man does *not* strive after happiness,' he wrote ; ' only the Englishman does so.'

It is not generally recognized how much of Nietzsche's intellectual make-up was derived from Christianity itself. His technique was first and foremost self-

L

accusation. Nietzsche is the intellectual questioning the value of the intellect, the decadent despising decadence, the human arraigning humanity before the whole animal world, denouncing him as the one animal who has had the hypocrisy to pretend not to be an animal, denouncing him as the one product of Nature who has sought to evade natural law.

In his preface to the *Case of Wagner* he writes :

'What does a philosopher firstly and lastly require of himself ? To overcome his age in himself, to become "timeless." With what then has he to wage the hardest strife ? With the characteristics in which he is just the child of his age. Well ! I am the child of this age, just like Wagner, i.e., a decadent. I am, however, conscious of it. I defend myself against it. My philosophic spirit defended itself against it.'

In the work of introspection the mind works something like the procedure of a court of law. There is no question of our being able to look placidly into ourselves and fish up 'home truths.' An unpleasant truth can only be discovered by a process of self-conviction which begins, as in a criminal court, with an accusation. And for this sort of work to be profitable that accusation, that self-accusation, must be something more than the mumbling of a form of words. Most of our emotions are ranged on the side of self-defence. There is, however, one very profound one—the sense of guilt, which can be convened to give force and sincerity to our self-attack.

Now there are many people to-day who are ready to pour scorn and venom on this sense of guilt. According to them it is no more than a cherished neurosis—a form of masochism. There are even schools founded to-day with the aim of bringing up children to be devoid of it, free from this blighting perversion. Much of this kind of work is, nominally at least, founded on Freudian ideas. But Freud's philosophy, though it may appear as an attempt to accept ourselves as we really are, is none the less highly introspective, self-accusing—it is a modern lay version of the confessional. And moreover, whether or not Freud has been directly inspired by Nietzsche, the Freudian school of thought would certainly have been impossible without that ferment, that dissolution of concepts, of which Nietzsche was the great instigator.

The philosophy of A. S. Neill may seem at first sight Nietzschean :

'The propensity to form ideals is the curse of old Adam. It is at the root of all religion, all education, all preaching of morals. Progress will follow the smashing of idealism, if that is ever possible. . . . For God's sake let the child be itself—an egotistical bundle of energy too much interested in its activities to do hypocritical things to please fathers and mothers.'

But such a point of view is not ' beyond good and evil,' *as Nietzsche got there*. It is rather a short circuiting, a seizing hold of the formula while neglecting the basis on which it rested. Neill's is an optimistic perversion of Nietzsche's philosophy. Nietzsche loathed optimism. In Nietzschean terms, Neill is the Englishman striving after happiness. For Nietzsche not only was self-accusation necessary to the development of the mind, but *all* affliction was admitted and even welcomed.

' It is great affliction only that is the ultimate emancipation of the mind. . . . It is great affliction only— that long, slow affliction in which we are burned as it were with green wood, which takes time—that compels us philosophers to descend into our ultimate

depths and divest ourselves of all trust, all good nature,
glossing, gentleness, averageness, where we have perhaps formerly installed our humanity. I doubt whether
such affliction " improves " us ; but I know that it
*deepens* us. . . . Be it that we learn to confront it with
our pride, our scorn, our strength of will . . . be it that
we withdraw from affliction into nothingness, into
dumb, benumbed, deaf self-surrender, self-forgetfulness
and self-extinction ; from such long, dangerous exercises
of self-mastery one emerges as another man, with
several *additional* interrogation marks—above all, with
the will to question henceforward more, more profoundly, more strictly, more sternly, more wickedly,
more quietly than has ever been questioned on earth
before. . . . Confidence in life is gone ; life itself has
become a problem.'

Indeed Nietzsche was above all the great questioner.
' One should not wish,' he said, ' to deprive the world
of its disquieting and enigmatical nature.' And what
he has handed down to us is not so much a doctrine as
a degree of sharpness and flexibility of inquiry such as
had never been attained before. We may go on to
attack problems of which he was only dimly conscious, but it is very difficult to get really out of the
range of his questionings. When we try to dig deep
we find the subsoil already loosened by his excavations.

' The most valuable knowledge is always discovered
last, but the most valuable knowledge consists of
methods.'

It is much the same with our knowledge of Nietzsche.
It is the methods which strike one most strongly in
the end. The more deeply one sinks into his works,
the more deeply one is led to regard them as comprising

a magnificent monograph on the art of intellectual excavation. He teaches us to question : he teaches us *how* to question. He teaches us, moreover, how to live with questions—we must be ready to face them and accept them, not seeking instantly to abolish them with an answer. How difficult, and perhaps dangerous, it is to *live with* a question is known to any profound psychologist. ' The desire for certitude ' says Wilfred Trotter, ' is one of profound depth in the human mind, and possibly a necessary property of any mind.' To subdue this profound desire was one of his ' dangerous exercises of self-mastery.' He was not a systematic philosopher, believing as he did that the will to system was a lack of rectitude. Philosophers who build systems have always one eye on this objective while they examine life. They thus fail to see its disquieting and enigmatical nature. With Nietzsche it was otherwise. With one eye on the world, the other was on himself ; and that inturned eye was quick to suspect the observer of bias, prejudice, dishonesty. With him self-mortification was an integral part even of the faculty of observation. In one of the aphorisms in *Beyond Good and Evil* we read :

' He who despises himself nevertheless esteems himself as a despiser.'

Here we have, as it were, the second order of introspection. The faculty of introspection becomes itself a subject for introspection. Man questions himself, and at the same time questions that questioning.

But, I shall be asked, is not the Superman a doctrine ?

Lo, I teach you the Superman.

The Superman is the meaning of the earth. And is not Eternal Recurrence a doctrine ? Yes, certainly they are doctrines, and pronounced with all the weight and authority of the doctrines of old. But I very much doubt if they are really living doctrines to any descendant of Nietzsche to-day. Oswald Spengler is typical in this respect : from Nietzsche he took his questionings, his *Fragestellungen* ; the rest he took from Goethe.

The Superman might be regarded as a crude and hasty application—an exaggerated application—of the theory of evolution. Evolution is essentially slow. After all, what is organic evolution but the transposition of our common notions of cause and effect to a different tempo—a time scale whose unit is not, as in physics, the second, but the interval between one generation and the next. It would be certainly not altogether untrue to regard Nietzsche's Superman in this way, but it would, I think, be still better to regard it as a romantic compensation for this terrible, this devastating self-analysis. There were times, even towards the end, moments of serenity, when he could live in peace in the clarity of critical thought. As late as 1888 he wrote to Brandes :

' To have understood that our European culture is a vast problem and by no means a solution—is not such a degree of introspection and self-conquest nowadays a culture itself ? '

But at other times, and they became more frequent, this weight was not to be borne, and then he decked out his Superman, regally, gaudily, with all those qualities that were exactly the reverse of all that he despised in man. Admittedly he does it beautifully, intoxicatingly, and in the glow of his romanticism we may perhaps for a while lose our critical faculties too. But not for long. The growing pressure of the machine age brings with it its daylight and steadily drives back the mists of all illusions. The Superman

is laid bare. We see him as a highly artificial thing—
a kind of negative of humanity in which every dark
becomes a light and every light a dark. We see him
as a dramatic, and even melodramatic figure, in which
the dissector and soul-diviner has disguised himself as
poet and prophet. As a figure set up *to shame man* we
see the Superman as a variant of the same critical and
corrosive process. The Superman is in the last resort,
another self-humiliation, another stick to beat the
wretched dog—mankind.

Or we might look at it in this way : Nietszche was
before all preoccupied by the problems of the individual
man. Now it seems to me that individualist philosophy
must be one of two things : it can be either lazy,
tolerant and pleasure-loving, or, on the other hand,
ambitious, that is to say, aristocratic. The first is
hedonism, a philosophy common enough in England.
The hedonistic view is, as we have seen, utterly foreign
to Nietzsche's nature ; but an aristocratic philosophy
developed in so intensely critical a mind could not
fail to be terribly exclusive. With its fine perceptions
it could pierce every pretence ; it could test, gauge
and discriminate with ever-growing severity until in
the end practically all mankind was put beyond the
pale. Such exclusiveness would lead him into an
intolerable position, the only escape from which would
be into an ideal world of his own creation.

Though wrapped up in all the warmth of romanticism and embellished by his brilliant literary gifts, this
aristocratic tendency in Nietzsche became more and
more truculent and strident. From the heights of
the Upper Engadine he stormed and scolded, sending
down volley after volley of contemptuous abuse to the
mediocrity of common man. Ordinary man, man as
a biological type, was rejected. Only the rarest of
exceptions were found worthy. Man who was at first

censured for being more than an animal was now reproached for being less than a god. He thunders at us grandly. There is no roll or rhythm known to thunder of which he is not a master. But it is rather sad, after the smoke has cleared away, to realize that the ' soul-diviner ' has become a drill sergeant.

In the first section of *Nietzsche contra Wagner* we read :

' I believe artists often do not know what they can do best : they are too conceited for that. Their attention is directed to something prouder than those little plants give promise of, which know how to grow up in actual perfection, new, rare and beautiful, on their soil. The final excellency of their own garden and vineyard is superficially estimated by them, and their love and their insight are not of equal quality. There is a musician who, more than any other, has the genius for finding the tones peculiar to suffering, oppressed, tortured souls, and even for giving speech to dumb misery. No one equals him in the colours of the late autumn, the indescribably pathetic happiness of a last, alder-last, alder-shortest enjoyment. . . . He draws his resources best of all out of the lowest depth of human happiness, and as it were out of its drained goblet, where the bitterest and most nauseous drops have at the end—the good or bad end—met with the sweetest. . . . As the Orpheus of all secret misery, he is greater than any one, and much has been added to art through him only, much that was hitherto inexpressible and even seemingly unworthy of art— the cynical revolts, for example, of which only the greatest sufferers are capable, and likewise many quite small and microscopic matters belonging to the soul, as it were the scales of its amphibious nature—yes, he is the *master* of minutiae. But he does not *wish* to be so ! His character loves rather the large walls and the audacious wall painting. He fails to observe that his spirit has a different taste and inclination—antithetical optics—and likes best of all to sit quietly in the corners of broken-down houses : concealed there, concealed from himself, he paints his proper masterpieces, which are all very short, often only one measure in length.'

The *tu quoque* argument always seems rather mean ; but, though I feel a little guilty in saying so, this rich description of decadence is surely at least as applicable to Nietzsche as it is to Wagner. Indeed, it is applicable to others besides—to D. H. Lawrence, for example, of whom it may not unfairly be said that he is most profound when he is most superficial. Nietzsche no less than Wagner loved ' the large walls and the audacious wall painting.' He too was a decadent ; but to quote again his own words : ' I defended myself against it. My philosophic spirit defended itself against it.' There is a heroic note in those words, a note of triumph. But was it not precisely here that he failed—failed, just as he says the artists often fail, to know *what he could do best ?* To have understood that he was a decadent, that was his great self-mastery, his self-abandonment. To have defended himself against that decadence, that was his capitulation to his own inner self-defence.

' Every age has its quantum of energy, a quantum determining what virtues are permitted to it, what virtues are proscribed. It has either the virtues of *ascending* life, and then it resists to the uttermost the virtues of descending life ; or it is itself an epoch of descending life, and then it requires the virtues of decline, then it hates all that justifies itself solely by plenitude, by superabundance of strength.'

In this he is completely mistaken. In fact, we can

now see that the exact converse is far nearer the truth. In an age when human vitality overflows, that is, in an age of violence, idealism will run to reason, gentleness, peace.  Only in a more civilized age, when reason has already undermined instinct, when thought has undermined action, only then will man ' discover ' vitality, and tend to idealize force, primitive instinct and desire.  The idealization of simple vitality is a sign that vitality has become—precious.  Man wants what he lacks.  Supply and demand !  High prices for rare products.  Nietzsche, the adept in self-consciousness, formulates the new ideal—unconsciousness. According to his *Three Metamorphoses* the spirit had lastly to become a child :

' Innocence is the child, and forgetfulness a new beginning, a game, a self-rolling wheel, a first movement, a holy Yea.'

But when once the spirit begins to think, begins to think about itself, it can never become simple and innocent again.  It can pronounce the ' holy Yea,' but in doing so it is giving its blessing to something it has learnt to envy.  This idealization of unconsciousness is in the end only another step in self-criticism—a self-consciousness itself.

How differently Nietzsche speaks in that aphorism in *The Dawn of Day* in which he says :

' The restless pursuit of discoveries and divinations has grown to us as attractive and indispensable as hapless love to the lover, which we would not at any price exchange for indifference—nay, perhaps we too are hapless lovers !  Knowledge in our hearts has developed into a passion which does not shrink from any sacrifice, and really fears nothing but its own

extinction. . . . Perhaps mankind may even perish
in this love of knowledge. Even this thought fails to
daunt us.'

Here he is in a very different mood, and seems to
realize that intellect is far more likely to bring us to
destruction than to integrate a new, stronger and
younger type of man.

And was there no possible solution to this conflict—
this conflict between ruthless self-criticism and its
romantic, heroic counterpart, this compensation in the
form of an idealized Superman which seems finally
to have dominated his mind? It is difficult to answer
such a question, and it can only be answered tenta-
tively. It seems to me that there was at any rate no
solution within the limits of individualistic thought.
But outside those limits? There are some indications
that his mind might at a relatively early stage have got
outside those limits once for all, in which case he would
never have needed a Superman at all. In *The Dawn
of Day* he writes :

' " The rule always seems to me more interesting than
the exception." Whoever feels thus is far advanced
in knowledge and one of the initiates.'

The idea here expressed, and which I shall never grow
tired of quoting, seems to me to epitomize in very noble
form the spirit of our scientific age. Of old, both
truths and values were proved by miracles, by the
extraordinary, the exceptional. But now we would
rather prove our case by showing it to be necessary,
to be ordinary, to be the rule. The desire for marvels
may still be with us, but it seems to us now a little
frivolous, even superstitious, to base any hope on the
exception. Had such an idea remained and taken root

in Nietzsche's mind he would surely never have become absorbed by aristocratic individualism, he would never have needed to make a demi-god of Caesar Borgia, he would never have craved for an ' art for artists—only for artists.'

Again in *The Dawn of Day* he is speaking in the same vein when he says :

' There is a profound and memorable saying, " Ce qui importe ce n'est point les personnes, mais les choses." This saying is like him who uttered it—great, honest, simple and tacit, just like Carnot, the soldier and republican.'

And yet again he says : ' We seldom have the courage for what we really know.' Did he ' really know,' even when he appeared to have forgotten it, that the rule was more interesting than the exception ? Did he ' really know ' what the saying of Carnot meant, and where it led ? Away from the Superman, away from man himself with all his individual doubts, troubles, problems ; towards mass movements, humanity in the block, towards economics, towards machinery.

But, as we have seen, there was one great obstacle to his going in that direction. It was his abiding contempt for happiness, which involved contempt and hostility to all political thought that had grown up round the concept of ' the greatest happiness to the greatest number.' That phrase and the whole philosophy of life implied by it, Nietzsche could never have accepted. It was utterly repugnant to him. But might he not have demolished that obstacle, and given socialism his own philosophy ? There was a task, a formidable task, but one which he of all men might have undertaken, and one that was worthy of his immense powers—the task of purging socialism of the quest for happiness.

I cannot finish without a word of warning. I should be very sorry if these words were to lead any one to think that he had got Nietzsche in a nutshell. I have mentioned the great range of Nietzsche's thought ; one cannot possibly do justice to it in so short a space. There are many other things to be said about this great philosopher, and many of them would no doubt conflict with what I have said here. And there is one thing about him which cannot adequately be told at all. That is the great fire burning in his mind. To know anything about that you must get close enough to feel its heat, and feel it keenly, either as a tingling excitement or, if you find him hostile, as a stinging pain. To look from a distance at Nietzsche's ideas—you cannot understand very much about him that way. One can understand very little about Nietzsche unless one brings one's own thoughts and feelings into sympathy or into conflict with his.

## XII

### KARL MARX

### (1818—1883)

### By A. L. ROWSE

WITH Karl Marx, the last thinker to be dealt
with in this series, we come up to and step over
the threshold of our own time. For there is no
doubt that great as was his importance to the nineteenth century, he is still more significant to the
twentieth century. Indeed there appear to be signs
that it is his outlook in thought which meets the
needs of our age, and so will come to influence its mind
more than that of any other single thinker.

This, however, has its disadvantages. It makes him
so controversial a figure, and the more difficult to deal
with adequately. His name is apt to be seized on as a
symbol by contending factions ; and the more dust is
raised in the conflict, the less clear it sometimes becomes what his views were and what exactly he stood
for. And yet we can all agree—whatever views we
set out with—that it is important to get down to
*understanding* this man and his work. Here we have
an enormous country like Russia inspired by his ideas ;
in every great country, France, Germany, the United
States, Great Britain, he has adherents, often important
parties in the State. And his purely intellectual in-

fluence—his influence on thought—is everywhere on the increase. What does it all mean? There must be some fire behind all this smoke. What is his contribution to the modern mind? What is its significance?

Certainly we must admit nobody was in a better position to make a contribution. The child of two distinguished peoples, the Jews and the Germans, he was in a singularly favourable position to imbibe from the sources of European culture : while circumstances brought him closely into contact with the life of nearly all the important countries of the West. Having spent the first half of his life in Germany, then the most fertile field of European thinking, and after some years in France and Belgium during the period of revolutionary upheaval around 1848, he came to settle in England where he passed the remaining, the longer half of his life. Circumstances drove him to England—we were then a refuge for the most distinguished exiles of Europe—but indeed he wanted to come ; he was anxious to study at first hand the most highly-developed industrial country of the world, the country which had created industrialism and the modern economic system.

Nor did he neglect to make use of all these varied influences bearing upon his mind : he brought all these strands together into a mental life, singularly rich and many-sided, to form a system of thought which yet was extraordinarily single-minded and concentrated in its aim. The resources he had to draw upon may be inferred from the fact that the thinker he most admired was Aristotle, and his favourite poets, Aeschylus, Dante, Shakespeare. The magnificent proud words of Dante, with which he closed the Preface to his great work *Capital* : ' *Sequi il tuo corso, e lascia dir le gente,*' were frequently on his lips, surprising as it may seem in a foremost exponent of socialism. But there were other elements too. From his father, a cultured and liberal thinker of the eighteenth century type, who read Voltaire and rejected the doctrine of innate ideas with Locke, he learned to look to sense-impression as the source of knowledge. Between father and son existed a mutual confidence very rare in degree. There is a remarkable letter which Marx wrote to his father, sketching out—as is the way with a young man of genius—his future plan of campaign, whatever risks it might involve, full of intellectual ambition, the will to know and to create, foreshadowing the whole programme of his life's work, and at the same time assuming his father's entire understanding—a rare expression of their mutual confidence.

The father was a lawyer, of the middle class, sufficiently well-to-do, employed in the Prussian civil service at Trier in the Rhineland. And here Marx was born on May 5th, 1818. In course of time he went to the University of Bonn, and then to Berlin, where he studied law for his degree, but gave the best part of his mind to history and philosophy. Having emerged at the end of his time with a doctorate, for a brilliant thesis on philosophy, he naturally looked to the academic world for his career. But those were years of reaction and repression in Germany then, as now : the Prussian Government had brought the elderly reactionary Schelling to Berlin, to succeed Hegel, and were driving all the most intelligent young men into opposition. Indeed, opposed to the militarist and junker Government, were all those by whom Germany's name was made famous in these years : the great poet Heine, Börne, Freiligrath, no less than the philosopher Feuerbach, and Marx himself. There was no way out this way, so he took to journalism and politics.

Meanwhile he had married : his wife was the beautiful Jenny von Westfalen, his friend from child-hood, the daughter of a Prussian noble, whose brother later on became one of the many reactionary Ministers of the Interior Prussia has enjoyed.

These were years of tremendous disturbance through-out Europe : in England the hungry 'forties were the time of the Chartist Movement—that revolution which failed to come off ; in France and Germany, Italy and Austria, there were constant upsurges of discontent, and the growing insistence of the middle classes to share power with the upper class, which led to revolu-tions all over the Continent in the year 1848. Marx—like all the most intelligent young men of his time —shared in the disturbance of mind. He was here, there and everywhere : making his name by writing in the Radical newspapers, linking up with others who were carrying on the campaign against the reaction, developing his views on politics and econo-mics, taking part in political activity. He was back in Bonn, then in Paris for a time, making the acquaint-ance of Heine and Engels ; then in Brussels working at his book, which was to formulate the new philo-sophical outlook, and for a few weeks even in London, reading in the British Museum—though a much greater landmark of this visit is the famous *Communist Mani-festo* which was composed here.

By far the most important consequence of this first period of activity was that he met and made friends with Friedrich Engels. From now on until their death they lived their lives in the closest intellectual collaboration. They had found—rarest good fortune —that they completely agreed in their outlook on the world, that they saw things in the same light and were as one in their objective. The co-partnership of Marx and Engels in their lives' work is one of the most

M

remarkable, and most moving, associations in the history of thought. Many people have found it difficult to explain their respective parts in the association, it was so close. Engels was himself a man of genius, very gifted and obviously of great charm ; he had considerable business capacity (for years he was the head of the family firm in Manchester, a branch of his father's cotton business in Barmen), an extraordinary aptitude for languages, and undoubted literary ability. The secret of the association was Engels' selflessness ; he recognized the greater genius in Marx and devoted himself to helping him in every way, not only supporting him financially but contributing his ideas to the common stock of Marxism.

Indeed, certain of the ideas originated with Engels, and he was the first to become a socialist—or communist as they called themselves. For all that it was a true partnership : during these formative years they hammered out together the foundations and principles which underlie modern socialism and communism alike, and are their contribution to thought. What were these ideas ?

The principle they worked out together—it marked a veritable revolution in thought—was *the principle of the unity of theory and practice*. (It is as well to give a word of warning here, in dealing with Marx's materialism. Marx was a philosophical materialist ; that does not mean in the least that he judged things from a vulgarly materialistic standpoint. So far from that, nobody lived a life of greater self-sacrifice and devotion to a cause than he did ; he threw over worldly success and even health and welfare, living in poverty and wretchedness, for the sake of the ideas he held. There are many so-called idealists who are altogether more ' materialist ' in the usual sense.)

This revolution in thought has to be seen against

the background of Hegel's idealism, which was the
dominant philosophy in Germany at that time, and
against which Marx and his friends were in revolt.
Hegel conceived of the world as Idea, and of the world's
evolution as the self-development of the Idea.  Marx
revolted against this self-enclosed world of mind ; he
wanted to break through to the real world of human
beings and their environment of the external world.
If you set out from the end of mind, he thought, you
end up with mind, never having penetrated through
to the real world.  Whereas the real point is to effect
the transition from mind to the actual world ; a transition which Marx effected with his principle of the
unity of thought and action, of theory and practice.

What this principle does, obviously, is to destroy
the independence of either thought or action taken by
itself.

There are two things the principle means.  The
first is that in fact *theory and practice are necessarily connected*.  There are few enough people who recognize
systematically what a clue to men's opinions you generally have in their circumstances.  They think what it
is to their interest to think, or rather what is suggested
to them by their environment.  The armaments
maker is the strongest of patriots—no doubt quite
sincerely ; the brewer is equally convinced that it is
good for our health that we should drink alcoholic
liquor, and so on.  There is no question of their
theory being independent of their practice ; it is part
and parcel of the whole complex of their views, their
interests and their relations to the actual world.  As
Marx says : ' The " idea " has always made itself
ridiculous in so far as it has been detached from
" interest." '

The second sense in which the principle may be
taken is *that theory and practice ought to agree* : that theory

M

should be related to action as a means to action, that
when it is unrelated to practice it leads to self-deception
and disaster.  We can all of us see how this holds good
from the side of action.  If you walk out into the
street with a different theory of the traffic from that
which is true to the facts, you will soon be eliminated
from the world of actuality.  That leads us to the
further consequence that the test is a practical one ;
as Marx says : ' the dispute concerning the reality or
not of thought, which is isolatĕd from practice, is a
purely scholastic question ' : and he holds that the
unity of the two is to be found in experimental science—
which seems a hard saying until one realizes that
practical politics is the experimental laboratory of
history, and that the social sciences are as much
sciences as physics and chemistry.

What Marx did, then, was to transfer the whole
emphasis which had been placed on ideas hitherto in
German philosophy, over to the world of nature and
men.  He saw men's ideas—their notions of religion,
metaphysics, law—no less than their views of society and
of themselves, as products of their whole social environment : he saw the history of these ideas as inseparably
bound up with the history of the whole society.  He
started from the world of real men ; ' realistic humanism,' he said, ' has no more dangerous enemy than that
speculative idealism or " spiritualism," which in place
of the real individual man sets up the consciousness or
mind.'  It is curious to think—what nobody has yet observed—how closely this anticipates and covers what
there is of value in the teaching of D. H. Lawrence.

But Marx took over from Hegel his conception of *the
process of development*—only applying it to the world of
historical fact instead of to the realm of ideas.

The idea of evolution, of growth and development,
was in the air at this time.  It was the whole spirit of

Hegel's philosophy : it was exemplified in England by Newman's *Essay on the Development of Christian Doctrine* (1845), years before Darwin's *Origin of Species* saw the light.   But the form in which Hegel conceived development took place appealed to Marx.   Instead of the slow, gradual process of evolution along one line of development, and in terms of the individual's struggle for survival, which we have become accustomed to from Darwin, Marx following Hegel thought of evolution as proceeding by contraries, by conflicts between opposites, and new reconciliations on a higher plane and in more developed forms.   If I may quote Lenin, Marx's greatest disciple, it is ' a development that repeals, as it were, the stages already passed, but repeals them in a different way, on a higher plane : a development in spirals, not in a straight line : a development in leaps and bounds, catastrophes, revolutions ; intervals of gradualness ; transformation of quantity into quality ; inner impulses for development imparted by the contradiction, the conflict of different forces and tendencies working on a given body or inside a given phenomenon or within a given society : interdependence and the closest, indissoluble connexion between all sides of every phenomenon (history disclosing ever new sides), a connexion that provides the one world-process of motion proceeding according to law.'

If I may add a word to Lenin—Marx's conception of evolution was both *social* and *dynamic*.   He saw that it was no mechanical process, but a highly organic one : and instead of thinking in terms of the individual's struggle for existence, he thought of the process as a social one, the struggle of the whole society apart from which the individual would not exist.   And thereby hangs a moral—it gives you the clue to Marx's social ethics.   Intellectually, the principle takes you straight back to Aristotle, the master of them that know.

Marxism is therefore, above all, a conception of society, laying bare the real forces at work in it, their modes of operation, its manifold processes of development. You no longer look to men's thoughts to give you the key to social evolution any more than you judge a man by what he says of himself : you look as a general rule to their material circumstances, i.e., fundamentally to the necessary relations set up between man and his environment in order that he may exist. It is a tremendous, emancipating conception. Marx's own account of the matter is given in the preface to the *Critique of Political Economy* (1859) : ' In the social production of the means of life, human beings enter into definite and necessary relations which are independent of their will—production relations which correspond to a definite stage of the development of their productive forces. The totality of these production relations constitutes the economic structure of society, the real basis upon which a legal and political superstructure arises, and to which definite forms of social consciousness correspond. The mode of production of the material means of life determines, in general, the social, political and intellectual processes of life. It is not the consciousness of life that determines their existence, but conversely it is their social existence that determines their consciousness.'

To the Marxist, once he has grasped in all its implications this conception of society *as a whole*, based on its real foundations of economic necessity and men's adaptation to it, and proceeding along the knowable, determined paths of historical laws—there is no going back on it : any other conception appears so superficial compared with it. But people are apt to think, because the process is a deterministic one, that man's role in it is purely passive. Nothing of the kind ; men make their own history, but there are limits to what they can do. The fact that there are limits is no discouragement to action ; in fact, in distinguishing between what is possible and what is not possible, it is the greatest aid to action. What man by taking thought for himself can add a cubit to his stature? You cannot, though you think as long as you like, think yourself off the map, or rather, though you may think yourself off the map, you remain on it. The real point is to know what is possible and what is not possible in society. To know how far you are bound by necessity —in that consists your freedom. It is by understanding those physical laws which make it impossible for man to fly that man has made it possible to fly. Marx has said : ' Freedom is the recognition of necessity. Necessity is blind only in so far as it is not understood.' Now you see why I called this conception of the historical process an emancipating conception. (But it is an historical process, remember. If you cast your mind back to Professor Macmurray's opening lecture, you will remember he says that we cannot understand the present unless we look to the past ; and that it is through understanding the past and the present that we shall be able within limits to forecast the future. Only fools fail to see how in this sense our outlook must be an historical one ; there was no greater bunk ever uttered than Henry Ford's dictum : ' History is all bunk.')

The basic form which social struggle takes, according to Marx, is that of the conflict between classes ; it does not often come into the open as armed conflict ; but it is always there, a struggle between classes over the division of the social product, wealth and property. It is the main motive-force in all social changes, colouring innumerable facets of social life where we should little expect it—prior even to the conflicts of nations, since classes are prior to nation-states, and national conflicts themselves a function of the class-conflict running horizontally through all society. ' The history of all human society, past and present, has been the history of class-struggles '—so runs the famous opening of the *Communist Manifesto*. ' Freeman and slave, patrician and plebeian, baron and serf, guild-burgess and journeyman—in a word, oppressor and oppressed—stood in sharp opposition each to the other. (They carried on perpetual warfare, sometimes masked, sometimes open and acknowledged : a warfare that invariably ended either in a revolutionary change in the whole structure of society or else in the common ruin of contending classes. . . . Modern *bourgeois* society, rising out of the ruins of feudal society, did not make an end of class antagonisms. It merely set up new classes in place of the old ; new conditions of oppression ; new embodiments of struggle.) Our own age, the *bourgeois* age, is distinguished by this—that it has simplified class antagonisms. More and more, society is splitting up into two great hostile camps, into two great and directly contraposed classes : *bourgeoisie* and proletariat.'

The struggle between these two is a struggle for control of the means of production, for, as we have seen, whichever class is in control of these can mould the social system after its own pattern and in its own interest. In another aspect it is a conflict over the distribution of the wealth that society produces, and according to Marx's analysis of capitalism, which is what his greatest work, *Capital*, is concerned with, it is the fact that labour constantly receives less remuneration than the wealth it produces which makes for the lack of correlation between production and distribution. The accumulation of capital from surplus value extracted from labour—i.e., all the wealth produced by it over and above what it receives back in wages—was, to Marx, the factor that lay at the bottom of the recurrent crises of over-production to which capitalism was liable ; and he forecast a gloomy prospect of more or less permanent crisis, unless society—or that class in society to whom he looked—took things into their own hands and made a fundamental change in the system. This fundamental change was the revolution to which he looked and which he regarded as inevitable. I mentioned earlier that his whole system of thought was single-minded and concentrated upon one aim— that aim was Revolution.

He was himself all for action. ' Philosophers have hitherto only interpreted the world,' he wrote early in his career ; ' now it is for us to *change* the world.' But these tendencies were not so fully developed in his own life-time ; and after the high-water mark of revolutionary activity in 1848, when Marx and Engels took part in Paris and Cologne, they retired to England, where the retreating tide left them high and dry for the remainder of their lives. Only on two occasions did he come again to the fore in practical revolutionary activity. In 1864 the International Working Men's Association was formed in London ; this was the famous First International, the parent of all the later attempts to draw together the working classes of the world into international association. Marx was the brain behind it ; and though his first attempt lasted no more than a few years, it was not only the precursor of the Second International, to which Western socialism belongs, and of the Third International of Lenin and the communists, but it laid down the lines which any attempt to found a new international order based on the working classes of the world must follow.

His last incursion upon the scene of European politics was on the occasion of the Paris Commune. This provided the fullest test of the sincerity and depth of his internationalism. There he was, a German faced with the issue of the Franco-German War. But if anybody saw the tragedy of it wholly and profoundly, it was Marx. The whole thing was a grief to him, and yet he alone, in the middle of war-twisted feelings, saw into the years beyond. When everybody else regarded Germany as an innocent victim of aggression, and France as deserving the awful catastrophe of 1870–71, when Carlyle was writing his fatuous letters to *The Times* defending the wresting away of Alsace-Lorraine, Marx was capable of seeing into the sorrow that lay beyond all that. He pleaded with his countrymen for justice, prophesying the awful retribution that always follows upon the heels of national war ; it was not mere prophecy, it was his profound historical judgement that spoke. And then, when the irreparable had been done, he rose to the height of true political vision when he wrote : ' *No greater misfortune can happen to a nation than to conquer another nation.*' If only Germany had seen that in 1871 ; if only other nations had seen it in 1918 !

But Marx—great genius that he was—was looking beyond nations, to the workers of the world. It is clear, when he called upon them to unite, that he regarded them as the only foundation for any secure international order.

# XIII

## SUMMARY

### By John Macmurray

WE have reached the end of our study of these Makers of the Modern Spirit. It is my task now to attempt a summary that will link the various chapters together and enable us to estimate what the whole development amounts to. So much that is interesting and suggestive has emerged that there is no very obvious way of doing this. No two people, I suspect, would choose the same way to do it. What I shall try to do is to give you my own impressions, confining myself so far as I can to what has arisen in the course of the previous chapters.

First of all let me refer to the chapter in which I tried to sum up the development from Aquinas to Newton. I pointed out there that the difference between the outlook of Aquinas and that of Newton lay in a different attitude to the world. Aquinas was interested in truth—that is to say, in the inner world, the world of the spirit. Newton was interested in the world outside him, its natural resources and the processes by which men utilized them. He was interested, that is to say, in the material world. The change from Aquinas to Newton is, therefore, a change in the direction of materialism. If you think this is a bad thing you must remember that it is the basis of all that we mean by modern progress. It is the basis of our scientific knowledge of the world we live in and of our control over it. I pointed out that this change was symbolized in the life of Luther. Up to a point he tried hard to force himself into the mould of the medieval world, to be like Thomas Aquinas. Then he rejected that effort and let himself go. He repudiated the traditional authority of the medieval world, threw off his fear and found himself free, facing the future. The result of this new freedom was that he began to live out into the world, and in consequence he set in motion revolutionary forces of change. In doing this he challenged authority in the name of his own freedom as an individual. The authority that he challenged was the authority of tradition. He found courage to be himself and to live from his own consciousness and not in subordination to the past.

Now, before carrying this story further I should like to ask you to compare two figures which have a certain similarity; I mean Aquinas and Goethe. The similarity between them consists in their universality. They seem to be eternal figures, not specifically and essentially related to their time, but significant for all time. The reason for that is their extraordinary wholeness and comprehensiveness as human beings. Their lives and their teachings have about them something that possesses the timelessness of a great work of art. On the other hand, just for that reason, they are peculiarly the expression of their times. They represent periods of equilibrium in the movement of human life. You will notice that they both flourished at the end of an historical period, that their perfection looks backward and forward at the same time. They sum up an epoch in themselves, and point the way to a new beginning. After them comes the deluge. Shakespeare holds a similar place in history, and so does Dante. Their

timelessness comes from the fact that they lived at
the crest of a wave which pauses and hangs balanced
just before it breaks. They are the flowers of a
season's growth within which lie the seeds of a new
season.

Now consider the difference of the two. Aquinas
sums up and expresses the Middle Ages. Goethe sums
up and expresses the first stage of the modern world.
The French Revolution is the obvious dividing line
between the two stages of the modern period. If we
can feel and express the difference between Aquinas
and Goethe we shall succeed in understanding the
difference between the medieval world and the first
period of the modern world. In the first place, we
notice that Dr. Gooch found it necessary to ask the
question : ' Did Goethe believe in God, and did he
accept Christianity ? ' It would have been ridiculous
to ask such a question about Aquinas—or about any
medieval, for that matter. For Goethe religion has
become a matter for questioning. He has a religion ;
but it is rather vague, very undogmatic and the result
of his own thinking and his own experience. In the
second place Goethe is a great poet rather than a
great scholar. That is not accidental. He is not an
intellectualist, though he is a man of great intellect.
Emotion has come into its own. He is much more
like Luther in that respect than like Aquinas, and
though he is on the side of law and order, a great
aristocrat, a believer in benevolent despotism, Dr.
Gooch has had to describe him as a moderate Conservative. He is, in fact, a humanist, and an individualist. He is, for all his aristocracy, a free individual
—in his thought, in his feelings and in his life. He is
full of reverence ; but it is not a reverence for tradition
or for established forms, but a reverence for Nature ;
and so he becomes one of the forerunners of Darwin

and evolution as well as one of the romantics. The implications of all this I must leave the reader to think out for himself.

Now let us return to the movement of the modern spirit. It is, we have noticed, a movement towards freedom. Now, freedom is primarily a negative idea. We can only seek freedom if we are enslaved in one way or another. The struggle for freedom is the breaking of bonds. One of the things that has struck me in reading the previous chapters is how much had to be said about what these men broke down and what they destroyed. They all destroyed something, and it was always something that masses of people clung to and held dear. (I am making an exception now of Aquinas and Goethe. The others are all destroyers.) Yet they are all makers of the modern spirit. It would seem, then, that on one side at least the progress of the modern spirit is a progress in destruction. From Luther onwards they all consciously or unconsciously destroy something. They are all revolutionaries, and what they destroy is an element in the tradition that lies behind them. Rousseau inspired the leaders of the French Revolution. Bentham destroyed privilege. Let me quote a passage from Mr. Jennings's chapter about Bentham. 'Above all what he did was to establish one fundamental principle. Social and political institutions must justify themselves. Privileges based upon wealth or ancestry or past depredations must be swept away. Human actions and human organizations must be submitted to the test of reason. If they fail to pass that test, and defend themselves by reference to history, the time has come for them to be swept away. That is the essence of the Benthamite position.' Darwin destroyed—without meaning to—the belief in the privileged position of man. Nietzsche destroyed the moral tradition and substituted a new moral outlook. Marx planned a final revolution to destroy most of what was left. The story of the development of the modern spirit is the story of an attack upon tradition and upon all authority that bases itself upon tradition. And to all people who believe in authority and discipline and the maintenance of tradition (and they are nearly always in the majority) that might seem the whole story. Most of those people, however, are in an ambiguous position. For the particular authority, or tradition, or privilege which they wish to defend has itself been secured or established by the process which destroyed the older traditions.

In fact, there is another side to the picture. These great men did not destroy traditions for the love of destruction. In many cases they did not even realize that they were destroying anything. They were fighting, in different ways, for freedom ; and the traditions and authority and privileges which they destroyed were simply hindrances to the freedom that they wanted. But freedom is a much more complicated thing than people are apt to suppose. The desire for it arises from a feeling of constraint. Something is preventing us from doing what we want to do. Immediately we feel that if only we could get free from that our troubles would be over. So we break loose, we destroy something and then discover that we are still in bondage to something else. In other words, people don't really know what they mean by freedom. They only know that they want to escape from something that oppresses them. And that is why the destructive and revolutionary aspect of the modern spirit is the first thing that strikes us. It has only been through a long process of trial and error that we have gradually discovered the conditions of human freedom. When a person asks : ' Why should I not do what I please ? ' the answer is : ' Because you can't.'

And that answer has two sides. It means first :
' Because you don't know how to.' It means in the
second place : ' Because there are material limits to
what is possible.' The first part of the answer means
that our *minds* are not free. They are governed by
habits from which we cannot break loose. And these
habits, whether habits of thought or habits of action,
are built into our minds by the pressure of the society
in which we are born. Tradition is simply social
habit. The first step in freedom, therefore, consists
in individuals developing in themselves the capacity
to rise above their habits—that is to say, above tradition—and to think and act upon their own deliberate
choice. They have to learn to decide for themselves
instead of doing things because other people do them,
or thinking things because other people think them.
That is a very slow process both in the individual and
in the history of human development.

But even if that were successful, it would only enable
us to know what we really wanted to do. It would not
necessarily make us free to do it ; because it might turn
out to be something which was not possible, because
we had not the power to do it. In the struggle for
freedom which has been the driving force of modern
development, these two aspects have always been
present. There has been a gradual freeing of men's
minds from the sheer weight of habit and tradition—
that is to say, there has been a gradual development
of individual initiative and a gradual extension of the
field of action in which it displays itself and in the
number of people who share in it. On the other hand,
there has been a gradual extension of our power to do
what we want to do—mainly through the increase in
scientific knowledge—and there has been an increase
in the number of people who have access to this power
which enables them to do what they want.

Now let us try to relate this to the development of the modern spirit as we see it in the men we have studied. If we compare Luther and Rousseau we find that they are both asserting their right to live their own life and to be themselves. But there is one great difference between them. Luther is asserting himself against the religious tradition of his time and is engaged in formulating a new set of religious beliefs. Rousseau is asserting himself against the political and social organization of his time and is seeking for a new form of society upon a new political basis. He wants, as he put it in his *Contrat Social*, ' a form of association in which each man, while uniting himself with all, shall remain as free as before and obey only himself.' He wants *everybody* to have the freedom which, at the time he was writing, depended upon being born into a privileged position in society. The idea of equal freedom for every one was his guiding idea. Of course, it was a revolutionary idea. It was the idea of democracy. It meant in practice destroying the privilege of the ruling classes and putting them on an equality with the common people. Everybody was to be free and equal. That was the demand that Rousseau made, and it ushered in the second phase of the fight for freedom.

But though Rousseau woke the spirit of democracy in Europe, he did little to show how this equal freedom was to be realized in practice. He was a romantic idealist. It is to Bentham, the hard-headed practical reformer, that we have to turn. Bentham distrusted the appeal to primitive instinct. He was all for reason and facts. He took rather a low view of human nature when he decided that it was pleasure, rather than freedom, that men wanted, and it is to Bentham rather than to any one else that we owe the sting in Nietzsche's gibe that it is only Englishmen who seek happiness.

But for all that he made a great contribution to the struggle for freedom. He taught the modern spirit to free itself from the feeling that social and political institutions were sacrosanct, and to look upon them as means to human welfare, justifiable only from the standpoint of their utility. He invented the idea of planning social and political life.

This idea of planning the reform of social institutions was immensely strengthened by the work of Darwin. He popularized the idea of evolution. The result was that people began to look upon the continual change of social forms as natural. They began to take progress for granted, and to expect that freedom and power and happiness and wealth should increase. They began to look for the golden age in the future, and not in the past. What is more important, they began to work for it as well as to dream about it. The more they worked, the more successful they were. Freedom began to come real in practice.

But there was a flaw in all this. The demand of the modern spirit had become Rousseau's demand for equal freedom for all. But the working-out of progress on Benthamite lines, though it resulted in the freedom of free trade and free competition, produced not equality but a rapid and glaring increase in inequality. The poor became relatively poorer as the rich became relatively richer. It became clearer and clearer that wealth was the key to practical freedom, whatever might be the truth about freedom of mind. So the struggle for freedom seemed to have changed into a struggle for wealth in which the weaker went to the wall. It had given us not freedom but a new and hideous slavery. It had merely resulted in the tyranny of the plutocrats, the dictatorship of wealth. The modern spirit was forced into a dilemma. Its struggle for universal freedom had destroyed authority, in

religion, in social and political life. And all that
freedom seemed to mean was the destruction of culture
and value in a violent scramble for material satis-
factions. Rousseau's noble savage had come into his
own and brought with him the freedom of the jungle.

Was it worth it ? That was the question. Should we
continue the struggle for freedom, when it resulted in
such frightfulness and destruction ? Or ought we
to call a halt, confess that freedom was a vain dream,
and retrace our steps before it was too late, before the
last remnants of civilization and culture were destroyed ? That dilemma, which is torturing all our
minds to-day, was foreseen by Nietzsche and by Marx,
and they gave opposite answers. Nietzsche decided
it was time to call a halt and save culture. So he
threw all his strength into the denial of equality.
Freedom, he said, is only possible for Nature's aristocrats. They alone are fit for freedom, and it is their
duty to assert their natural right against the masses.
Nietzsche stood for an aristocratic revolution against
the destructive tide of the democratic movement.

Marx, on the other hand, refused to despair of
humanity. He reasserted the demand for freedom
and for equal freedom for everybody. He realized
as clearly as any man the horror of the last stage of the
fight for freedom. But he refused to turn back. He
was no more of a dreamer than Bentham. But he
believed that in science and the scientific spirit he held
the clue to the future, and that the struggle for freedom
and equal freedom against the authority of wealth
would prove the final assault by the forces of freedom
against the citadel of the enemy. He set himself to
plan the final victory, like a general marshalling all his
resources for the decisive attack. The great fight of
the modern spirit, he thought, the fight for human
freedom, will not be won outright until it is won on

the economic field. If it is won there, he believed, it will be the final victory.

If we look into this carefully, we shall recognize that Nietzsche and Marx represent the two horns of the modern dilemma that is now facing us. The struggle is defining itself as one between Fascism and Socialism. Nietzsche is the protagonist of Fascism, because Fascism wishes to call a halt in the struggle for freedom and go back to the old idea of authority and discipline, to the old Roman tradition of Europe from which the modern spirit has been in revolt. It wishes to save culture from the final onslaught of the demand for equal freedom. Marx is the protagonist of Socialism, for Socialism reasserts the faith in freedom and equality, and demands that we shall not call a halt and retrace our steps, but carry the struggle through to the bitter end. It is between these two that the modern spirit has got to make its choice.